EASY LIFE

From chaos to calm with minimal effort

ROSIE BARRON

GW00659489

The Tidy Coo

Published in 2021 by Tidy Coo Books

ISBN Paperback: 978-1-7398750-0-8

Ebook: 978-1-7398750-1-5

Published with the help of Indie Authors World

www.indieauthorsworld.com

IndieAuthors
World

Acknowledgements

I'd like to thank my husband, Ian, aka Mr Tidy Coo, for being my rock and captain of my cheerleading team. My children, Beatrice, Max, Tabitha and Felicity, for being helpful, understanding and self-sufficient whilst I wrote this. Natalie, who along with Ian, was proof-reader extraordinaire. My most amazing photographer Laura, for making my home and possessions look stylish in these photos - she worked miracles at short notice. As did my fabulous designer Nikki – she saw inside my head and produced my cover. My mother Lesley for rocking up when I needed her. My family and friends who supported me in this and forgave me my absences. The team at Indie Authors World for being the ones who got this book out there. Finally, my lovely clients for welcoming me into their homes; I couldn't have done this without you.

Chapter 1

Introduction

Why Organise?

You've picked up this book, so I'm guessing that you are interested in getting organised. But why? Why should we bother getting organised? Why waste all that energy in the first place if the goal is to live an easier life?

To me, getting organised is not about living in a rainbowed Pinterest Perfect house, or living an Insta-worthy lifestyle, or in minimalistic monastic simplicity.

No, getting organised is about getting rid of those things that hold you back and weigh you down, so that you can get out and enjoy your life. It is about freeing yourself from the drudgery of looking after your home so that you can focus on the more important and interesting things. It's about taking control of your life and living it the way that YOU want to.

I'm not here to tell you the "right" number of spatulas to have in your drawer, or how many dresses you should have in your wardrobe, or how many books you should have on your shelves; instead I'm here to give you the tools so that you can decide that for yourself. Avoid prescriptive lists telling you what you should and shouldn't have; tempting as they are, they don't take into account your individuality. Every person in this world is an individual, and every person will need or want a different number of belongings.

Whilst professionals may use the Clutter Image Rating Tool objectively when we are concerned about health and fire issues, for most people clutter is subjective. Decluttering and organising our homes is less about removing a certain number of items from each category, and more about taking control of our home and life. Like many animals, even if we are put in a "perfect" space, we like to nest and make it our own. It is about how much control you feel you have over your own space rather than how others perceive it.

When we feel that our environment is out of our control, we can feel stressed and anxious. Our cortisol levels rise and over time this can make us more susceptible to mental health issues, such as depression and insomnia, and physical health issues such as heart disease.

As well as impacting our physical and mental health, when our environment is disorganised, we end up wasting time searching for our lost belongings and wasting money replacing those that we can't find. The fewer things we have, the fewer things there are to go wrong and the easier it is to maintain the things that we have. The easier things are to maintain, the more time it frees up for us to do our own thing.

Don't waste your precious time looking for lost things, or looking after things that you don't need.

Don't waste your money buying things that you don't need.

Don't waste your valuable space storing things that you don't need. Your home is a home, NOT a storage facility.

"What is it you plan to do with your one wild and precious life?"

Is my own home always tidy? I'm asked this a lot and my answer, when I've finished laughing, is that I have four Home-Educated children, five dogs, three cats and a couple of tanks of fish in my home, with eight horses, four bunnies and assorted poultry in the back garden. Some days it looks like a tornado has swept through a school, a library, a toy store, riding stables and a pet shop and then deposited the contents in my living space. But give me twenty minutes and everything will be tidy again, and tidy not by using the Squirrel Method (whereby you sweep everything off the surfaces into a bag and squirrel it away in the cupboards, never to be seen again), but with everything returned properly to its place. My house is "Deeply Tidy" – although on the surface it can get untidy, you can go into any cupboard and you'll find it organised.

However, I am not a naturally tidy or organised person. I'm not a superwoman who can run on zero sleep, or who has miraculous energy levels, or staff to help me run my home. I'm just a normal person who has had to find ways to stay on top of my very full life.

I procrastinate, I get distracted, and a lot of the time my head feels like it's filled with gunk. I leave things until the last minute because I think I have more time than I do, and then I skid in sideways with a "Phew, I made it!" expression on my face.

Believe me when I say that if I can do this, you can too.

I am not one of these people who will constantly exhort you to live a life that is 10/10 – I'm quite happy living a 7/10 life. I don't want to be a millionaire, or run a marathon, or fly to the moon. I just want to live a life where I am not wasting my time looking for my keys, or wasting my space storing stuff that doesn't support me, or wasting my money replacing stuff that I can't find, or mindlessly buying things I don't need. I like to lead a laid-back, easy life, where I have time to be with my family and ride my ponies, whilst doing a job that I enjoy.

Getting organised DOES require an upfront investment of your time and energy (and sometimes your money too), but as Benjamin Franklin said, "For every minute spent organising, an hour is earned".

It may be that, during this book, you come across some advice that you don't like. In which case, feel free to ignore it – this is not a one size fits all book; some people will love it and I am sure that there are some people out there who will not. The advice in this book is based on what I have found works for me and my clients. I can't, of course, address every single scenario that I come across in my work in the course of one short(ish) book or bring in every bit of my experience. If I did that, it would be the size of an encyclopaedia. Instead, I am trying to give you the tools to work on your own.

Similarly, if you try to get started and don't succeed, please don't beat yourself up. If everyone were able to do this on their own, I wouldn't have a thriving business. So much of what I hear every day when people are speaking to me is shame and embarrassment and I say, "You know this is totally normal, right?" I'm in houses all day, every day where, for whatever reason, people have become overwhelmed.

If you do need in-home Professional help, then as a first port of call I would suggest APDO (the Association of Professional Declutterers and Organisers) in the UK or the KonMari website worldwide. Other countries have their own associations, such as NAPO in the US. I also run online courses which many people have found to be a very successful halfway house between trying to do it on their own and getting in one-to-one help.

If you decide that the advice in this book isn't for you, then I won't be offended – if you are already living an Easy, joy-filled and happy life, then that is brilliant. However, if you are stressed, or tired, or feel overwhelmed or unhappy, then do give it a go. You never know, it might just work...

Using this Book

I have set out this book in the order that I usually find it the easiest to work with clients. You can do the categories in whichever order you prefer, with the one proviso that you start where you find it the easiest. Make sure that you have read the Introduction, Golden Rules, Vision and Pre-Decluttering sections before you start.

Many people are tempted to start in the kitchen, but I would caution against this as the kitchen is actually a trickier (and more overwhelming) category than you might think. I usually encourage people to start with clothing and the reason for this is that clothing is worn daily, it's close to the skin and, despite being absolutely opposed to Fast Fashion, in the event that you do make a wrong decision, it is usually relatively easy to replace an item.

Once you have done your clothes, I recommend moving on to other things that you wear, such as coats, shoes and bags, then on to toiletries and cosmetics, then linens and cleaning products, before starting to tackle other categories such as the kitchen. I have grouped the various categories around the rooms where I would expect to find them so that I can make specific storage suggestions.

However, just because you do not have a utility room does not mean that you can skip the utility room section! You will almost certainly have the items that I mention in the utility room. Similarly, if like me you don't have a loft, that is no reason to skip the loft section; most people have seasonal decorations and suitcases.

I like to leave paperwork until the latter part of the journey because I have found that it is a category that many people get bogged down in. People find it stashed throughout their home, in underwear drawers, down the back of the sofa, stuffed in a bag in the cupboard, and it is only once we have gone through the majority of the home that we find it all. As you find paperwork around your home, put it into the Paperwork Box that you will set up as part of the decluttering preparation (unless it is obvious rubbish, in which case, simply discard it).

If you find Memory objects as you tackle each category, please don't get caught up trying to decide what to do with them. Instead put them to one side and address them when you have had more practice.

Worksheets and Other Resources

As you work through the book, you will come across exercises to do and worksheets to guide you. I know that many people do not like to write in books, or will be working from an e-book, so I have included downloadable worksheets on my website for you.

www.thetidycoo.com/worksheets

You can also find videos of folding demonstrations on my website, and I regularly share motivation, top tips, videos and other useful information on my social media platforms.

The Case for a Pre-Sort

I like to work in categories because I find that it is the easiest way to do things – bring a whole category together (even if it's just your socks!) so that you can see how much you have, sort it out, then store it in one place.

However, in some of the homes that I have been in, we need to do a good pre-sort before we get started, particularly if some members of the household have been keen on the "Squirrel" method of tidying. If this is you, don't fret! Go through those boxes and bags, sort the contents into categories, discard the obvious rubbish and easy decisions and then store the categories together ready for a proper go-through.

Working with Others

One of the most frequent questions that I am asked is, "How do I get my partner or children to tidy?". There is only one way to do this. Lead by example. Focus on your own journey first and other people will follow, usually with a satisfying inevitability! However, do not even consider trying to push others into getting tidy and organised until you are able to be so yourself. Do not push or nag someone else into getting their space tidy, especially if your own space is not there yet.

When I go into people's homes, I do so by agreement and never by decree. I don't ninja roll into your home and throw everything out, I go where I am invited. I'm not bossy (much) and I don't have a top-down rule because being ordered about is no fun for anyone and imposing a system on someone else simply doesn't work. Imagine if I steamrollered into your home uninvited and started pushing you around, telling you to do this and get rid of that. How would you feel?

I almost always work with women, often mothers, and sometimes when I enter a home I am met with scepticism and, occasionally, outright hostility from their partners. However, I always promise not to touch anything that belongs to them and almost invariably, at some point during the process, as they see the benefits that are accruing, the partner will sidle into the room and mutter, "Err, could you just give me a hand to organise..." and we're off! Even those who don't come to me personally to ask for my help will start to show me the work that they've done on their own. It really is amazing, but my

experience has shown that it ONLY happens if they are not coerced or nagged into doing it.

If, by the time you have done your own things, they truly have shown no inclination to get organised and their belongings are impacting your life, then it is as well to designate a space that is their own so that they can order it exactly as they wish. Remember that this is a partnership and we all have to make space for each other in this life. I get a bit frustrated with the amount of cookware in my home as my husband is the chef, but then he gets frustrated with the number of ponies in the garden...

This same advice applies to children. I have included a section on working with children, but it is important to remember that children need autonomy and control over their space too. We need to teach them the skills of how to tidy and organise themselves, but we can't do that if we have not learned those skills ourselves too. Do your own journey first before you tackle your children's rooms.

Hoarding Disorder

"I'm a bit of a Hoarder" is a phrase I frequently hear and usually my response is, "No, you're not." You may live in a cluttered and disordered home, but Hoarding Disorder is a diagnosable Mental Health issue, often caused by past trauma. I will not work with people who say that they want to "stage an intervention" for someone else. It has to come from the person who has the disorder. You cannot simply go in and clear the hoard as this is traumatic and counter-productive. People with Hoarding Disorder need therapy and kindness, not shock and shame.

It is a long and slow process, and we go step by step, ensuring that each step is accepted before moving on, gently unpacking feelings and emotions as we go. With one of my lovely long-term clients, it took 18 months to get to a point where she was comfortable with me discarding a receipt that was over 7 years old without checking with her. But step by precious step, we make progress.

If you or someone you know is affected by Hoarding Disorder, in the UK, the best place to start is Hoarding Disorders UK. They have a great Ice Breaker form on their website which you can fill in to make it easier to talk to a Health Professional.

Chapter 2

Golden Rules

Start with your Vision

Declutter First

Choose Positively

Go for the Easy Wins

Work in Categories

Handle Everything

Release with Thanks

I trained in The Marie Kondo Method with Marie and have since spent many hundreds of hours working with clients and running workshops. I am constantly learning, not only from other Professional Organisers both formally and informally, but also from my clients. From this, I have developed my own set of Golden Rules that I have found work in pretty much every situation.

Start With Your Vision

There is a reason that Vision work is included in almost every self-help book, be that a book about Time Management, Business, or Organising and that is because it is such a powerful tool. Knowing where you want to be is a strong motivator and usually the people who have the most successful decluttering journeys are those with the strongest vision. The next chapter is given over entirely to this, so I won't say too much about it here, but you have to know where you are going and what you are trying to achieve.

Declutter First

Do not buy storage solutions until you have decluttered! I cannot stress this enough. Organising alone will never lead to an easy life, so never try to organise what you can discard. I have seen organisation systems worthy of a museum where either the items sit in stasis, never used, or (as is usually the case in children's toys) the owner is driven nuts trying to maintain it. When I work with my clients in-home, by the end we usually have a stack of unused organising systems that we have unpacked and decluttered!

I often have people ask me how they can keep an area tidy and the answer is Declutter, Declutter, Declutter. The fewer things you have, the easier it is to keep them organised. If your space is still becoming untidy easily, then you still have too many things. Continue to declutter until it is easy to live in your home.

I feel I should reiterate here that I am in no way a minimalist. I don't live in a minimalist box. I don't have minimal possessions. I don't have a home that is perfectly tidy at all times. What I do have is a home filled only with the things that I love and that support me in my life. You should not be surrounded by stuff that doesn't serve you, and there is no point at all in organising that stuff. Declutter first.

Choose Positively

Choose what to keep because you love it and it supports the life that you want to lead, rather than because you don't know what to do with it. I see a lot of people keeping things, "just because" or "just in case" or "because someone gave it to me". None of those are good reasons for keeping things. "Just in case" hardly ever happens and your everyday environment and living is more important than "some day".

Decide what it is that you want to be surrounded with. Initially don't get distracted by where you want your discards to go; just decide whether or not you want to keep them in your life. I'll provide questions you can ask yourself to help you make those decisions.

Choosing positively what to keep rather than negatively what to discard drives an entire mindset shift. We cannot be happy by focusing on the things that we don't like; we can only be happy when we focus on the good things. Things that will support you in the life that you want to lead.

Choose to keep things because you love them, or because they are used. When I start in people's homes, we usually start with clothes as the easiest point and I get people to pick up one or two of their favourite items and tell me about them. They often smile and I see their hearts lift. These are the things that we are aiming to keep!

Now, of course, some things may not make your heart lift with their beauty, but practical objects definitely have a place in our homes too. The electricity bill may not make you happy when you receive it, but living in a home with electricity almost certainly will.

Go For The Easy Wins

Don't worry about the harder decisions initially, especially not the sentimental ones. The more practised you become at letting things go, the easier it is. By the time you get to the harder decisions, they won't feel so hard any more. Some people want to crack straight on with a high stress area. I am against that.

When we learn to swim, we don't jump straight into the deep end and try to swim the Channel, because then we need rescuing, or worse, we drown. Instead, we start by paddling in the shallow end. Finding our feet, learning how the water moves and how it will support us. As we get more confident, we learn to float and then to move ourselves, always with the back-up of being able to touch the bottom if we need to. By the time we hit the deep water, we're confident in our ability to swim and can positively revel in our ability to turn somersaults and dive down to the bottom.

So it is with decluttering: don't worry about what you're going to do with the difficult decisions until you are well-practised with the easy ones. Don't start by worrying about what to do with Great Aunt

Betty's tea set, instead start with something simple, like your sock drawer.

When you are decluttering and you come across a decision that is hard, put it to one side and move on to an easier decision. Do not allow yourself to get blocked by the harder decisions; come back to them later on, when you've had more practice, and you will find them easier to make.

Work In Categories

Working in categories really is the easiest way to make progress. Categories can be as large or as small as you want, but much easier to get all your notebooks together and go through them, than to try and do a shelf, keep a notebook because you need it, then keep another on another shelf. I once had a client who had 13 pairs of nail clippers and who had no idea that she had that many until we ferreted them all out.

As I said in the Introduction, sometimes it's good to have a general pre-sort and declutter of anything obvious, but when you are making "proper" decisions, it definitely helps to work in categories. It prevents churning, which is the movement of things from one space to another when you can't quite decide what to do with them.

Handle Everything

Often my clients look at me somewhat askance as I dive into yet another cupboard and pull the items out into the light, but I am doing nothing that I haven't already done in my own home. It really is important to make sure that you handle everything. "I've been looking for that!" is one of the most uttered phrases that I hear when working with clients.

When I'm working with clothing, I'll often have people say things like, "Oh no, I don't need to do the socks, they are all fine", but when I persuade them to do so, they let go of about half because they realise that those socks have holes, or are not in pairs, or are uncomfortable. Whilst it can feel like rearranging the deckchairs on the Titanic to go through a sock drawer when the rest of the home is in disarray, by doing one drawer and freeing up space, you'll do another drawer and free up space, and before you know it, you've got loads of space.

Release with Thanks

It can be hard to let go. Even following all the rules here, easiest first, working in categories and so on, not every decision will be easy. People often have an issue with having spent money on something that hasn't worked, or clothes they don't like anymore, or with letting go of gifts that people have given them. In these situations, I encourage you to be thankful to the object for whatever it has done for you and you will often find that this makes it easier to release it.

For example, maybe you bought an expensive dress that has never quite fit right. You're not going to get your money back on it if you leave it stuffed in your wardrobe. Be grateful for the lesson it has taught you: in this case that nothing should enter your home unless it ticks ALL of the boxes.

If someone has given you something as a gift, remember that the job of a gift is to show love and respect. It's not very respectful of that love if you leave a gift stashed in a cupboard unused. Release an unwanted gift to be used by someone else, you're only giving away the physical object, not the love that came with it.

Storage

I know how tempting it is to run out and buy storage solutions to organise your stuff, but many of the homes that I work in are overflowing with storage solutions that are absolutely no use at all. During your initial tidying and organising, use whatever you have to hand.

Don't waste time finessing storage solutions when you are part way through your journey, because you will find that spaces open up within the home as you go along. I remember being asked, "Surely the kitchen storage doesn't affect the bedroom?" and my reply was, "Oh you'd be surprised!". You might find an extra space in your wardrobe that you then transfer something into from the porch, which then opens up space there for something else and so on. Don't lose your decluttering momentum by becoming distracted by storage. Once you have decluttered your belongings, if you want to, you can buy nice storage.

Here are a few tips that you can use as you go along:

- When deciding where to store something, ask yourself where you would look for it. Make sure that it is easy to put away, because whilst we will always go somewhere to get things out, we are much less likely to make a journey to put things away.
- Put your systems where the things pile up. I do my girls' hair in the kitchen, so the kitchen is where the hair bobbles are kept.
- Always store like with like. It really is the easiest way. Don't have all your things muddled in together, divide them out so that they are easier to find.
- File fold and store vertically. If you think about bookshelves, we always make sure that we can see all of the spines so that we know what is what. It is the same when we are storing anything: don't leave it piled up so that you can only see the top item, store the objects so that you can see them all. I have videos on my website where I demonstrate how I fold clothes and other things.
- Make use of vertical storage. I will often put shelf risers into tall spaces and look for unused spaces on the backs of door that can be used.
- Keep surfaces clear. Try not to store your items on the work surfaces. Make use of the space under the surface or on the wall. If things are in your way and you need to move them to use the surface, then you're wasting your precious time.
- Avoid boxes with lids. Almost always, things will get left on top of the lids rather than being put away. A drawer is (somehow!) much easier, or an open basket.

Introduction and Golden Rules Summary

- Getting Organised is about making life easier

- Do your own things first

- Don't throw away other people's possessions without their agreement

The Golden Rules are here to guide you:

- Start with your vision

- Declutter first

- Choose Positively

- Go for the easy wins

- Work in categories

- Handle everything

- Release with thanks

Storage solutions

- Where would I look for this?

- Easy to put away

- Systems where the problems are

- Like with like

- Store vertically

- Use vertical storage

- Keep surfaces clear

- Avoid lids

Chapter 3

Getting Started

So, you're ready to start Decluttering and Organising, all set for a brand-new start. But where do you start? To be successful in anything that you do, it helps enormously to know where you are going.

The Wheel of Life

The Wheel of life is a useful tool to illustrate how balanced your life is at this moment in time. To use it, you look at each area and mark on the scale how satisfied you are in that part of your life, where 1 is extremely dissatisfied, 10 is extremely happy. The idea is not to score 10 in every segment, but to have a relatively balanced circle. The areas with the lower scores will indicate those parts of your life that you might choose to focus your energy on changing. Fill it in now, before you start your decluttering journey, and then fill it in again at the end to see the difference.

Purpose – Contributions through work and volunteering

This is how you feel that you contribute to the world. It doesn't have to be work, it can be anything where you feel you make a difference. For me, the focus in this section is on the way that I help other people with my work, and also the education of my children.

Health – Physical, Mental and Spiritual wellbeing

How are you? Are you happy? Sad? Tired? Brilliant? What is your physical health like? Do you eat healthily and do enough exercise? When I first filled this in, years ago, I was exhausted with pernicious anaemia, was definitely drinking too much and eating junk. It was the lowest scoring area and as the rest of my circle was relatively evenly balanced, I had to spend time improving this so that my wheel was more circle like and less like Pac-Man.

Lifestyle – The manner and environment in which you live

Are you happy in your home? Do you feel like you have control over it? Are you happy in general with how you live? Often this is an area where my clients score is low and we have to see how we can balance out the circle so that they are happier.

Relationships – Your engagement with others

Not just a relationship with a significant other, but also with friends, family and work colleagues. My husband and I try to make sure that we walk the dogs with each other most mornings so that we can download to each other and talk without distraction and I have a set-in-stone date with two of my friends once a week. Having these times carved out and in my diary makes a huge difference to my life.

Development – Personal growth and learning

Time spent learning, about yourself and the world around you is always well spent. I spend a lot of my time reading, particularly about decluttering!

Play – Activities for amusement and delight

Play doesn't have to be swinging around on the monkey bars. For me, play is time spent with my horses, or watching a movie with my kids. Things that you do just for your own enjoyment.

The Wheel of Life

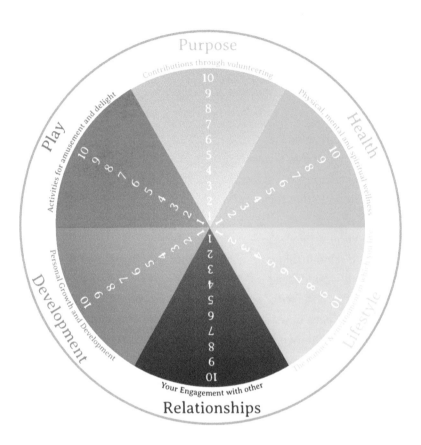

I am not
Organised
because I
have Time,
I have Time
because I am
Organised.

– Rosie Barron,

The Tidy Coo.

Vision

As part of setting up for a successful declutter, you will need to work on your vision, which is how you want your life to look. Imagine I could come in and wave a magic wand: what would your home look like? What would it feel like? What would it smell like? Of course, your vision can, and will, change over time, but it's your vision right now that I want you to consider and record.

There are several ways that you can work on your vision. Some people like to make mood boards, whilst others like to write it down. However you choose to do it, you will need to take some time to do this. Pick a quiet spot and make sure that you have set aside half an hour or so to think about this. Focus on your most perfect day and talk yourself through it. What would happen when and why? For example, start with what you see when you wake up. Think about it in minute detail and write it down in all its glory. How do you feel at each part of the day? Visualisation is a strong and powerful tool. It's important to focus on a positive vision: "The surfaces are clear and easy to clean", rather than the negative, "There is no clutter."

My own vision starts with as much a feeling as anything else. Warm and welcoming is how I want my house to feel. Somewhere the kettle is always on and there is cake in the tin to share. Somewhere it is safe to sit and talk, where you know that you're supported in your lows and celebrated in your highs. Somewhere where the energy may get very high at times, but where there is always an underlying calm and stability.

Some of my clients have been buried in their lives for so long that they've forgotten what it is that makes them tick. I've had clients who have found the idea of imagining a lovely life to be quite confronting and scary. But you are allowed to dream of a world where you have the time to pursue the things that you want to do. You are allowed to dream of a life where you have a home you can be happy in. You need to dream it to be able to do it. As I scribble this, sat at the kitchen table after a morning of lessons with my children, before a call with a client, I never thought that I'd write a book. This book would not have happened without dreams and a vision of what I want my life to look like.

Throughout this book you will come across worksheets like the one on the following page. Fill them in to guide you through the process. Larger copies are available to print out at

www.thetidycoo.com/worksheets

Vision Worksheet

What words come to mind when you describe your home?	What words would you like to come to mind when you describe your home?
What works well in your home?	What doesn't work well in your home?
What are you grateful for in your home?	What would you like to change in your home?
What do you talk about when you socialise?	What do you spend most of your money on?
What do you love to do?	What do you spend most of your time doing?

Imagine that you have completed this journey already and that your home is decluttered and organised. You've released everything that doesn't serve and support you. Close your eyes and imagine coming through your door. Take your time as you mentally walk through each room. Open each cupboard and look at the finished product. How does it look? What do you see? What does it feel like? Describe it in the box below, going on to additional pieces of paper if needed. Then describe your perfect day – again detail is good here, so take your time and use as much paper as you need.

Describe your decluttered and organised home.

Describe your perfect day.

Preparing to Declutter

Exit Strategy

A word about waste.

We only have one world, there is no Planet B. We should declutter as mindfully as we can and I have a sustainability section on my website for this reason. However, I also want you to think about the fact that once something is made, sooner or later it is going to end up in landfill, even if it is reused or recycled in the meantime. The only way to stop something ending up in landfill is for it not to be made in the first place and the only way that we can do that is to take away the market for it. Whilst we may want to make sure that every single thing we have goes to the right home, sometimes you have to just accept that it is going in the bin. Use your feelings about this to stop yourself buying more in the future. Buy once and buy well.

Selling your discards

There are many ways that you can get stuff out of your home, and selling is one of them. It can be tempting to try to get back some of the money that you have spent on items, but do make sure that it is worth your time. Remember the amount of time you will need to spend taking photos, listing, responding to enquiries, getting the item packaged and posted and so on. Not to mention that it will be sat in your home taking up space and making it difficult to move on until it is sold and dispatched. If you definitely want to sell an item, give yourself a deadline to have it gone by. When I am working in home with a client, I usually ask them to have anything sold before I come back for another visit. If it is still there when I visit again, then we donate it instead.

Declutter kit:

• Pens – for labelling	• Bags/Boxes for:
• Post Its – preferably fully sticky	• Bin
	• Recycle
• Scissors	• Donate
	• Move room
• Cleaning products	• Paperwork Box
• Cloth	• Sentimental Box
• Water (with product if desired)	• Travel Box
• Hoover	

Pre-declutter Worksheet

Investigate three Charity Shops you can donate to:	Investigate a Shelter or Refuge and find out what products they take:
Where in your home will you store items to be: • Donated? • Recycled? • Sold?	What is the address of your local refuse/recycling centre? Do you need to book?

Chapter 4

Wardrobe

Clothing

I like to start with clothing and accessories. A good wardrobe declutter always makes you feel accomplished.

To get started, find one or two of your very favourite items of clothing and pick them up and think about when you last wore them. How do you feel when you hold them? When I'm working with my clients, I will often find that they smile when they are holding something that they love, so pay attention to yourself and remember that we are making positive choices. These favourites can be anything from a ball dress to a pair of favourite tracksuit bottoms, as long as they make you smile and your heart lift. Hang these favourite items up where you can see them and use them as a reference point during your wardrobe declutter.

Next, gather together a category of clothing – if you are feeling brave, you could get every single item out of your wardrobe and your drawers, but if you are not, just work your way through the category list in the worksheet at the end of this chapter. Make sure that you take out all of the items in each category so that you can see how many you have. You really must handle everything! Don't make the mistake of looking at your sock drawer and thinking, "Oh everything in there is fine" because shortcuts like that are not the way to a truly

Easy Life. Remember, it's an investment of time and energy now to free you up in the future, both physically and mentally.

The first thing you must ask for each item is if you really love it and love wearing it. If you do, that's a winner, so put it in the keep pile. Remember to go for the easy wins first; look for the things that you love, or things that you're really not sure at all why they are still in your wardrobe. In this very first flurry of activity, don't get caught up on one particular item; if you can't make a decision in about 10 seconds, put it to one side and choose another, then come back to it at the end.

A lot of people say to me, "If I got rid of everything that I don't like, I won't have anything to wear!" I say, if you don't love it, you're probably not wearing it. You can have a wardrobe filled to the brim with clothes that you don't love and you'll find that you are only wearing a very small percentage of them. So have a go anyway, remember that I'm not going to ninja-roll into your home and take away your discards, you have complete control over this. If you pick only the clothes that you love, and you put them neatly back into your wardrobe and then decide that you don't like the way that it is so easy to use, then you can put some of the clothes that you discarded back into it. The chances are though that, once you've seen what it can look like, you'll not want to go back.

Of course, you can choose to keep items for practical purposes. If you are not very fond of a uniform that you might wear to work, but you need it to do a job that you love or that earns you a living, then of course, you need to keep it. Or if you have an activity that you love doing, but the clothing for it doesn't make you particularly happy, then focus on what the clothing enables you to do. Equally, some-times we need to hang on to an item until we can replace it with something that we DO love. For example, when I first started decluttering in a positive fashion, I had a few things, like my horse riding gear, that I didn't feel good in, but horse riding is an activity that I love. So I hung on to those clothes. Over time, I have replaced them with items that I do absolutely love.

Once you've picked off the easy wins, it's time to delve a little deeper into those that you're not sure about. As you pick up each individual item, here are some questions that you can ask yourself. Does it fit well and do you feel good in it? When would you wear it? If you have clothes that don't fit, check them anyway, because I have found that people tend to put clothes that don't fit into boxes without checking them. Unless you are pregnant or had a baby in the last year, I would suggest letting go of clothes that are more than a dress size away.

I have been everything from a size 10 to a 20, back down, back up and now I'm steady at a 14/16. What I noticed when I lost weight after having children was that all these clothes that I had been hanging onto in the hope that I could one day get back into them – literally dragging them around the world – no longer suited me or my lifestyle. They clung in the wrong places and sagged in others.

If you are on a weight loss journey, or planning one and do end up losing weight, treat yourself to some new clothes! If you gain weight, also buy new clothes – I have been slowly going up the dress sizes recently, but I'm not hanging onto my size 12s; let them go and make someone else happy. If I want to lose weight, I'm not going to do so by shaming myself looking at the teeny tiny dresses I used to wear.

People don't change habits through shame, but through love and connection.

If you feel unhappy with your body and feel like you don't look good in anything, let me tell you now, you are wrong. Firstly, we are our own biggest critics – the things that you are worrying about are probably not even noticed by anyone else. Secondly, everyone can look good in clothing, it's just a matter of finding out what suits you. Whilst I am a great fan of the school of thought, "How to get a Bikini Body? Get a Bikini, put it on your Body!" I am also aware that not everyone is body confident. However there are ways that you can dress to enhance the things that you like, whilst minimising the bits that you don't. After four big babies in quick succession (the last one was 10lbs3), my stomach is no longer the washboard that it once was – and that's putting it kindly. So I tend to wear higher waisted skinny jeans that flatten my stomach and draw attention to my legs instead. That said, when I explode into a room, no one is looking at my stomach anyway, they are too busy trying to keep up with the invariably energetic conversation I'm trying to have...

I did a wardrobe declutter with one of my lovely clients (I do love my clients, I get very attached to them!) who had a wardrobe that was full to bursting – in fact, it had burst. There were clothes filling up almost the entire room and she had no idea what was in there. As we went through the process, it became obvious that she had been holding on to clothes that were too small. She didn't like the fact that she had, for one reason or another, gained weight, and so she was holding on to all the clothes that she had previously fit in to.

After a chat, we decided that she was going to release everything that was over 2 dress sizes away, and check the rest. She was amazing – everything that was in the smaller sizes went and even a fair amount from the sizes that she was close to. She realised that even if she got back down to those sizes, there were things in there that she didn't want to wear.

In the end, she released 20 black bin bags of clothes. Some went to the rag bag, some went to charity, some she sold as bundles on Social Media and some got sold individually. By the time she had finished, she had a great wardrobe with clothes that she loved and she could see, and the mental load of having clothes piled all around her room was lifted.

Show yourself some love. Release the clothes that don't fit you to someone who can and will wear them, and buy yourself some clothes that make you happy. This doesn't have to be instant, take your time to find clothes that you truly love rather than seeking an instant fix. Remember you will now be able to use your new ability to choose items that truly make you feel amazing. Use the chapter on Capsule Wardrobes to make a mindful shopping list.

Some other questions that you can ask yourself are things such as, if this was in a shop, would I buy it again? Imagine it hanging on a rail, would you even look at it? If you tried it on in the changing room, would you take it home? When was the last time that you wore this item? Sometimes we do like things, but we never reach for them because there is actually something else that we prefer. Is it damaged? How many of this type of item do you have and how many do you need?

Another lovely client of mine had a large number of black leggings. She could never find them, so she kept buying more. Once we had brought them all together, she could see that she had rather more than she needed. She discarded the ones that were damaged and then looked at the ones that were still wearable. We put them in order of most favourite to least favourite, decided how many she actually needed, counted down the line and let the rest go to charity.

While you are absolutely welcome to try on the clothes you own, if you're having to try on every item, it's clear that you've not been regularly wearing them and you should ask yourself why.

Sometimes I get people say, "I don't know!" and my answer is, "What would the answer be if you did know?". Now this sounds like a funny question, but often, people do actually know the answer in their heart, they just don't want to admit to it.

If, after all these questions, you are still really uncertain, then keep it and do so with confidence. Put it in your wardrobe in an easily accessible place and see if you wear it. Do not shove it into the back, never to be seen again, but make sure you see it daily. Then revisit it in six months time and make the decision then. Sometimes we have to live with less for a while in order to see that we can live with even less. I do a quick wardrobe check in the Spring and Autumn to see if anything needs updating or replacing and this is a good opportunity to revisit any pending decisions.

Don't fall into the trap of saying, "Well it cost a lot!" You're not going to get your money back by leaving it in your wardrobe. That money is already spent. Let the item go. It is such a pity for things that are made to be used to sit abandoned in a cupboard! If it is something that cost a lot, you could see if you could sell it, but, as I said earlier, give yourself a definite date that if it hasn't sold by, then give it away.

Don't let your wardrobe wear your clothes!

Learn your lessons and be thankful for them. We all make mistakes when we buy things and the important thing here is give yourself grace. Perhaps you bought that boho dress thinking that you would float around the fields in it, but you realise that you are actually a wellies and jeans sort of a person, or perhaps you bought that smart suit that's actually too severe for you. Be grateful for the lessons that these items have taught you and release them with thanks. Equally, perhaps you have an older piece of clothing that you adored wearing, but it's done its job and had its day. If you take a moment to thank it for its hard work, it will be easier to let it go. Release it to move on to the next phase of its life cycle.

If you come across any items in your wardrobe that still have labels on and are staying, take those labels off! Welcome the item of clothing into your home properly.

Finally, there are no right or wrong numbers in this. I might only have three pairs of shoes, but I have eight ponies: I'm not in a position to tell you that you have too many things! Only you will know the right number for you.

Handbags

I like to start the Accessories section by having a handbag declutter (and please bear with me if you are someone who doesn't use a handbag)! There's a statistic out there that women spend 81 days of their lives looking through their handbags for things that they have lost. This is also a favourite activity of mine to do when I'm giving talks, as I get everyone to empty out their handbag, sort through it to see what they want to keep in it and what can be removed. I think the best ever find was when someone from the WI pulled out a whisky miniature. Other interesting finds have included a rotting satsuma and a spoon that was supposed to be in the kitchen.

Take everything out of your bag, and ideally locate every single other bag in your home and empty them too. This is one of those categories in particular where I hear, "Oh I've been looking for that!". Jewellery, make up, medication – all sorts of things turn up. Empty the bags, sort the contents into categories, discard the rubbish, put away the things that need to be put away, and then return to the bag anything you need to take out with you.

It seems to me that there are two types of handbag people out there. One is like me, only really using one handbag on most occasions. I have one that I like and that goes with practically everything, so I don't swap and change that much. I have a handbag insert that I use for those rare occasions when I do swap bags. I leave the insert in my bag, but I do take out anything extra that I have accumulated during the day, such as receipts.

The other type of handbag user tends to have more bags and swaps between them frequently. Regardless of what type you are, I like to set up a handbag station near the front door. It's a place for unloading your bag when you come in and helps to make sure that you always have everything to hand when you leave your home. This system also works for people who use their pockets instead of a handbag as you have a place to empty your pockets as you come in.

Back to the declutter: once you've emptied all your bags, it's time to take a look through them and see which ones you want to keep. I used to have a lot of handbags, but over time I have realised that, for me, it's too much effort to regularly change them over, so I mainly stick to one. It then seemed like a waste of space and money to keep extras in my wardrobe, so I released them to people who would actually use them.

Shoes

Like handbags, I used to be a bit of a shoe fiend. I guess that as my weight oscillated, shoes were something that I knew would always fit and so I tended to collect them. I loved to wear skyscraper heels and would squeeze my feet into shoes that were far too narrow. When I was a young teacher, I used to happily do playground duty in 6-inch stiletto heels! However, as time has gone on, I have to say that I have become more discerning about what goes on my feet and I now insist on wearing shoes that are beautiful AND fit correctly. I have fewer pairs, but because I now go for quality over quantity, they last longer and I can wear them with anything. I have one particular pair of beautiful heels that get brought out whenever I have a smart occasion, and I know that I can run for a bus or train or flight in them!

There are reminders of the questions that you can use to ask yourself in the summary, but one of the questions that I find particularly useful when doing accessories is, "Is it comfortable and easy to use?"

We've all had that lovely bag that falls off our shoulder, or those gorgeous shoes that we can't walk in. If it's not easy or comfortable to use it, you are unlikely to reach for it. Shoes or handbags that are uncomfortable for you may fit someone else perfectly, so don't waste the space in your home, release them.

Other Accessories

Use the same criteria and workflow for coats, hats, scarves, gloves, belts and jewellery. Do check the pockets of coats before donating them!

Building a Capsule Wardrobe

Having decluttered your wardrobe, I want to talk about mindful shopping. I've labelled this "Building a Capsule Wardrobe", but that doesn't mean that I think that everyone needs a tiny wardrobe, or that anyone's wardrobe should look like anyone else's wardrobe. There are no right or wrong numbers, only the number that is right for you but, in order to make it easy to get dressed, it helps to have pieces that mix and match. I can, almost, pick up anything in my wardrobe and wear it with anything else. There are a few things that don't go – perhaps they are too close in colour, or pattern, but in general, I could get dressed in the dark and still look presentable. Capsule needn't mean a monotone either, my wardrobe is full of lovely colours.

My expertise here is as a Professional Declutterer and Organiser, not a Style consultant. I do often recommend to my clients that they have their Colours and Style done because I have found that it saves time and money. I am a Blue/Leaf Autumn and a Dramatic Natural-Classic. It means that when I go shopping, the first thing that I do is to scan the shop for colours that I know suit me the best. Once I have spotted them, I go and check out the item and I look to see if the style is likely to suit me, such as pattern, neckline, material. Only if it ticks those boxes does it come into the fitting room with me, and only if it makes me feel amazing does it come home with me. It has definitely saved me a lot of time and money!

I have put this table together to show you how some of the pieces in my wardrobe go with others. I have included a copy in the worksheets for you to fill in yourself once you have decluttered. If you need more copies, they are downloadable from my website.

			Bottoms				
Tops		Green shorts	Wideleg Trousers	Jeans	Flower Skirt	Short dress	Midi Dress	Long Dress
	Teal T-shirt			✓	✓			
	Purple T-shirt		✓	✓	✓			
	Striped T-shirt	✓		✓				
	Mustard Long-sleeved	✓		✓	✓			
	Marine Long-Sleeved	✓		✓	✓			
	Teal Cardie			✓	✓	✓	✓	✓
	Mustard Cardie	✓	✓	✓	✓	✓	✓	✓
	Green Jumper			✓				
	Purple Jumper	✓		✓				

Once you have filled it in, look for gaps within your wardrobe that need filling. Make a note of any useful pieces that it would be good to buy and then, if you are out shopping, rather than impulse buying things that don't fit into your wardrobe, look for things that help to fill in the gaps. For example, if you have a skirt that can't be worn with anything else, when you are out shopping, look for a top that will go with it (and ideally will also go with another bottom layer).

If you have a large wardrobe, you could consider downloading one of the wardrobe organising apps that are out there, but the idea is to develop your wardrobe into one that makes it easy to get dressed in the morning rather than making you sigh in frustration.

When it comes to Clothes shopping, where you spend your time should tally with where you spend your money. In the worksheet, you will find a time circle to fill like the example below. Fill in the circle with how you spend your waking hours over the course of a year. Include Work, Home, Social, Hobbies, Holidays, and any other activity that takes up a chunk of your time. The chart is split into 12 segments, but that is just to give you a marker.

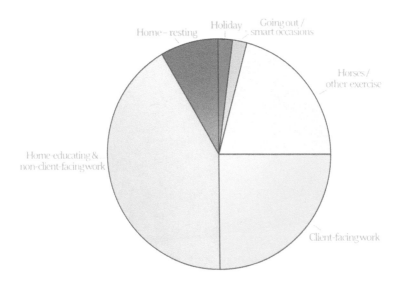

Your budget should reflect how much of your money that you spend on each of these categories. If you spend 50% of your time at home, you should spend 50% of your budget on things that you wear in the home. I spend a whole heap of my time riding, and my budget reflects that. I invested in a really good, high quality coat and I have not regretted it, although at the time I went rather pale at how much it cost. However, my cost per wear of it now is pennies, because I wear it so frequently.

When shopping, look out for good quality clothes. Things to look for are natural fibres (although there are some more modern artificial fibres that are good quality too), generous seams and hems with patterns that match at the seam, good quality fastenings and material that is cut properly – so that when it is hung the seams go straight down the side. Buy once, buy well.

Finally, just before we finish up, if you wear one, do consider getting yourself professionally fitted for a bra. I use an independent Bra Fitter who is close to me and she is excellent. Great stock, prices very reasonable and wonderful service, so do check if you have one in your area.

Wardrobe Summary

Things to remember:	Questions to ask:
• If you don't love it, you won't wear it	• Do I love this?
• Check everything, even if it doesn't fit	• Do I need it for practical reasons?
• Release clothes that don't fit	• Does it fit?
• Be thankful for the lessons	• Is it comfortable?
• Take labels off	• Do I feel good in it?
• There are no right numbers	• When did I last wear this?
• Make a handbag station	• Would I reach for it?
• Release unwanted gifts	• Is it damaged?
• Check pockets before donating	• How long have I owned this?
• Aim for a capsule wardrobe	• How many of these do I have?
• Make a mindful shopping list	• Which is my favourite?
	• Would I buy it again?
	• Does this belong in my travel/holiday box?
	• Is it worth the real estate?

Clothing Worksheet

How do you feel about your current wardrobe?	In your ideal life, what clothing do you wear?
What works?	What are your favourite items?
What needs to change?	What do you need to keep for practical reasons?

Capsule Wardrobe Planning

	Bottoms							
Jackets and Tops								

Time Check

Spend your money where you spend your time.

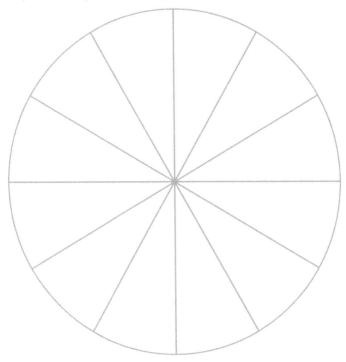

Mindful Shopping list:

Clothes and Accessories Checklist

Clothing	Accessories
Tops	**Footwear**
o Long sleeved	o Shoes
o Short sleeved	o Boots
o Vest tops	o Flats
o Jumpers	o Heels
o Cardigans	o Sandals
Bottoms	**Coats**
o Skirts	o Light
o Trousers	o Heavy
o Jeans	**Hats**
o Leggings	o Warm
o Shorts	o Dressy
Dresses	o Fascinators
o Day	o Light
o Evening/Occasion	**Scarves**
Other	o Warm
o Uniform	o Light
o Active wear	**Handbags**
o Swimwear	o Day to day
o Nightwear	o Evening
o Loungewear	**Jewellery**
Underwear	o Necklaces
o Pants	o Bracelets
o Bras	o Rings
o Socks	o Earrings/Other piercings
o Stockings & Tights	**Other**
o Vests	o Belts
	o Umbrellas

Wardrobe Storage

Do not break your heart over clothing storage at this point! Storage solutions can and will change throughout the process, so try to avoid spending money until you know what you are keeping. What follows are some tips and options for storing clothes and accessories for you to consider.

When putting items away in drawers, I prefer to file fold them so that they are more easily seen and I use smaller boxes to corral clothes within larger spaces. File folding means that they take up less space too. Check out my website for videos that show you how to do this. I fold everything that looks happier folded, and hang the rest, although the balance between folding and hanging for you will depend on your storage space.

I will admit to a weakness for matching velvet hangers! I love the way they look and I like the way that clothes don't fall off them. Slim-line hangers mean that the wardrobe is less crowded, but I know people who prefer the bulkier wooden ones because they take up more space and so prevent them from buying extra clothes. Do whatever works for you, but matching hangers make all the difference when it comes to how a wardrobe looks. I now leave the hangers that come with the clothes at the store so that the store can reuse them.

There are several ways that you can choose to hang your clothes. Some people like to hang by length, others by colour. Personally, I like to hang by type, putting like with like so that it is easy to see how much of something I have - again, find out what works for you.

> *Top Tip: To prevent a floordrobe, have a hook in your cupboard where you can put your half-worn clothes. For example, I might put my riding kit on for a few hours and then shower and change -- I don't want to put my riding kit away into the drawer, but neither do I need to wash it just yet, so I hang it on a hook inside my cupboard where I know that I can find it.*

I am often asked if I rotate my wardrobe seasonally. Now personally I don't, firstly because I don't have that many clothes and I have enough space in my wardrobe for them all, and secondly because I live in Scotland, so I wear my winter clothes pretty much all year round! On the few days of the year that it is warm enough for me to wear summer clothes, I don't want to be faffing round looking for them in storage somewhere. However, if you have a small wardrobe and rotating works for you, then go ahead and do it.

I like to make a "Travel Box" with my clients. Into this box goes anything that you only use when on holiday. I know that some people have sets of clothes that they only wear when they are away, so I suggest that you gather all of those together into one place and store them separately from the rest of your clothes. As we go through the rest of your home, we'll add other things to this box with the intention that you will then be able to pack to go away with minimal effort.

On a day to day basis, my regular handbag lives at the top of the coat cupboard. Bags other than this are stored stacked inside each other in my wardrobe. It is easy to pull out the one that I want and put the others back into the stack. If your bags are being kept above your eye line, then having the handle or strap showing over the top is useful for remembering them.

Shoes are best stored out of their boxes because boxes take up so much space, but this is not a hard and fast rule. You could consider those Z shaped organisers or an over-the-door hanger. If you do store your shoes in boxes, make sure that you stick a photo on the front. This will save you the time and energy of hunting through each box to find a specific pair.

Storage in Entryways and Porches

Some of the items that are mentioned in this chapter, such as shoes and coats, may be stored where you enter your home rather than in the wardrobe. Unless you are blessed with a fantastic mudroom, and let's face it, not many of us in the UK are, the porch or hallway can become a rather crowded place. This is one area where I do recommend seasonal rotation. Keep as little as possible here, only the items that are in daily use rather than general storage.

Use vertical storage where you can, and keep shoes off the floor with racks or boxes. I make use of vertical storage for my hats and gloves, with a hanging organiser fixed to the inside of a cupboard where I can see what I have at a glance. My scarves are file-folded neatly into a box on a shelf so that I can see what is there.

If you have children, make sure that there are some hooks within their reach so that they can hang up their own coats. I have a box where their scarves and gloves get thrown into.

Remember that it should be easy to put your things away because if it is not, then they will just end up hanging around and cluttering up the entrance to your home.

Clothes and Accessories Organisation Summary

In the Wardrobe:

- File fold to maximise space
- Smaller boxes are useful in larger spaces
- Matching hangers create a streamlined look
- Hang your clothes according to colour, length or type
- Have a hook inside your wardrobe for lightly worn clothes
- Create a Travel Box
- Stack handbags inside one another
- Store shoes out of boxes
- Look for vertical solutions, such as over the door hangers
- If using boxes for shoe storage, ensure that there is a picture on the front of the box

In the Entry:

- Create a handbag station
- Only store daily use items here
- Keep shoes off the floor
- If you have children, ensure that they have hooks at their height

Bedroom

The primary function of a bedroom is sleeping and it should be set up for that. Sleep is so incredibly important: it protects both your mental and physical health, improves your ability to learn and retain information and helps you to think more clearly. A calm bedroom improves your chances of getting a good night's sleep.

As far as possible, ban tech from the bedroom. I've never had a TV in my bedroom as the blue light disturbs sleep patterns. Black out your room as much as possible and keep it cool, but not cold. Keep the sides uncluttered and bedside tables/nightstands free from piles of books. Make your bed every morning!

Bedroom Worksheet

How do you feel about your bedroom?	Describe your ideal bedroom.
What works?	What activities currently take place in here?
What doesn't?	What activities do you want to take place in here?
What needs to change?	

Entryway

Whilst it may seem a little odd to jump from the Bedroom to the Entry, many things that we store in the entry are part of the clothing and accessories categories, so it does make sense to think about them at the same time.

Entryway Worksheet

How do you feel about your Entryway?	Describe your ideal Entryway.
What works?	What is currently stored here?
What doesn't?	What should be stored here?
What needs to change?	Where can you set up a handbag station?

Chapter 5

Self-Care

Toiletries are anything used to keep yourself clean and fresh. Items like shower gel, shampoo, sanitary products, deodorant, moisturiser, face scrubs, lip balms, body wash, shampoo and conditioner fall into this category. Collect all of them into one place and put them into categories.

There are a couple of different things to consider when we are doing toiletries. Firstly, "Is this something that you use?". The number of products that fill bathrooms that are simply not used is amazing. Perhaps you bought it and tried it once, then realised that you didn't get along with it. Perhaps it was a gift and it's not something that you would use, but you haven't liked to get rid of it.

Whatever the reason, if you don't use something, it should not be taking up vital space in your home, especially in this most crowded of rooms, the bathroom. If it is something that is open, then usually I just dispose of it, washing it out and recycling the container. I know that some people use bits and pieces to clean with instead, but that's a decision for you to make. If it is unopened, then consider donating it to a refuge or similar.

The second thing to consider is how long a product has been open. Many products have a time frame within which they should be used once opened, which is shown by the little open box symbol on the packaging.

Often this can be a safety issue: for example, sunscreen starts to degrade once it is opened and using sunscreen that has been opened too long could lead to skin damage. Sometimes bacteria can grow in opened bottles and then will be transferred to your skin when you use the product, and sometimes, the product simply isn't as effective or doesn't smell as good if it has been open too long. If you have several products that you use, but don't use fast enough to get through within the use by time frame, consider buying smaller sizes in the future. Sometimes we buy larger sizes because it seems like it is better value for money, but if you are not using the entire product within the time frame, then it is a waste.

Top Tip: Keep a permanent marker pen on your shelves to label opened products with the date that they were opened so that you don't lose track.

Sometimes there are things that make you smile that are not used. For example, I was bought some lovely bath salts. Now I don't use anything in my bath other than water as my skin is incredibly sensitive, but I love the packaging and I like seeing them on display. Don't feel that you have to discard just because. Look for the things that bring you happiness daily.

I often discover lots of travel sized bottles taken from hotels in my clients' homes when we are clearing out bathrooms. Some people like to take them away on holiday with them, and others like the idea of this, but never actually do so. If you have a set of hotel bottles for this purpose and you really don't want to discard them, I suggest relocating them to your Travel Box that I talked about in the chapter on clothing. The next time that you go away, see if you use them. If you do, then that's great. If you don't, then release them and make sure to leave them in the hotel next time. I have a set of refillable bottles that I use for travel that I fill up with my favourite products to travel with.

Once you have been through your toiletries, give some thought to future use on the theme of sustainability. There are some very simple swaps that you can make, such as replacing plastic toothbrushes with bamboo ones, going with products that have less packaging such as shampoo bars, or changing your brand of toilet paper to a more sustainable one. There are lots of companies offering these kinds of sustainable products now and many donate part of their profits to charitable enterprises, such as those that help build toilets for those who don't have them.

These small changes won't save the planet on their own, but zero waste is not about one person doing it perfectly, it's about everyone making small changes. Don't be afraid to make small changes because you are worried about not being able to make the bigger ones. Make the smaller ones and the bigger ones will come.

When it comes to storing the toiletries that you are going to keep, there are some who suggest removing them from the shower or bath each time you use them and putting them into a cupboard. Personally, for me that is too much effort. I'm just too lazy to keep getting them out and putting them away. However, I only keep a minimum number of products in the shower as I keep my regime very simple and easy.

I do, however, try to keep surfaces in the bathroom clear and any products tidied away in my cupboard after I have used them. It helps reduce visual clutter and keeps cleaning to a minimum.

Cosmetics

Onto cosmetics! As with every other category we cover, your end result will look very different from the next person's. There is no right number for this, only the right number for you.

Start by collecting all of your make up supplies together. This might mean rooting it out of handbags, travel bags, the bathroom, the hallway, your bedroom, the car etc. Categorise it into lipsticks, mascaras, powders, eye shadows and so on and then take a good look at it. Which of those items are your favourites? Which do you reach for on a daily basis? How about when you are going out? Those are the ones you want to keep. Let go of the others, even those that cost a lot of money, but you don't use because they weren't right. You may not want to let them go because they were expensive, but you're not going to get your money back with them sitting in your toiletry bag! Take it as a lesson learned.

The other thing to remember is that, like toiletries, many items of make-up have a use by date on them and it is important to discard them once they have been open longer than this date. They can grow some quite nasty bacteria on them, so it's important to let them go, especially as they are being used on your face and near your eyes. Like the toiletries, consider keeping a permanent marker with them so that you can label when they were opened and know when you should discard them if you use them infrequently.

I don't have much make-up as I'm too lazy to bother wearing it often, but many of my clients choose to keep quite a lot. Once again, it's important to remember that this is a very personal choice and there is no right or wrong. One of my 12 Weeks To Tidy Workshop attendees had a bit of an epiphany whilst doing make-up. She had a lot of it because she felt that she ought to. However, as we tidied, she realised that make-up wasn't really something that interested her, and she ended up letting go of most of it. She kept a few bits for special occasions, but felt incredibly liberated by this decision.

Whilst we're here, don't forget to give your make-up brushes a good clean. It should be done with lukewarm water and an antibacterial soap. Also at this point, make sure that you go through all the bags that you use to store your make-up. Do you still need all of them? Are they in good condition? Do they need a clean? Don't rush out and buy new ones though, use what you have until you have finished decluttering.

Hair

Hair accessories covers everything you use to look after your hair, from dryers and straighteners, to brushes and clips. Gather them all together in one place as usual and sort them into categories. Ask yourself if you use each one and if it is something that adds value to your life. Whilst I would never push someone to discard something that they are uncomfortable discarding, I would like to do a little reminder here that it is always easier to look after and organise fewer things.

There are so many different ideas on storage that I'm not going to go into it too much here. What I will say is that everything needs a place, and that place needs to make sense. With three girls (and one boy), we have quite a few hair accessories! The hair elastics are communal and are kept in a box in a kitchen drawer along with 2 hairbrushes – one for straight hair and one for curly hair. These are kept in the kitchen because that is where we do hair every morning and whenever we find spare bands hanging around (they seem to shed them everywhere!) we know where to put them back to.

Nail care

With nails, it's obviously the same as with the other categories. Bring all your nail care products together, categorise and then go through the categories. Check that old nail varnishes have not gone gloopy and remember to ask yourself those important questions including, "Which one do I reach for?"

A Make Up Station with a mirror, good lighting and somewhere comfortable to sit is a good idea.

Relaxation

Relaxation covers all things relaxing, so candles, oils, oil burners, massage stuff and so forth. I won't repeat my usual instructions; you know what to do. Just be aware that in this category there may be many gifts; remember you don't have to hang on to them just because they were given to you. You can hand them on.

Medicines

This is often quite an easy and satisfying category. Collect all the medicines together from wherever they are around the house and sort through them. Are there any that are out of date? How about half-used prescription medicines? Or medicines that you no longer use? Let them all go. It is not unusual for my clients to find that about half of their medicines are out of date. You can dispose of medicines at your local pharmacy.

Once you've been through the medicines, you need to decide if your current storage is the best way for you as a household. There are so many different ideas out there as to how you can store medicines. Some people like to label up lots of different boxes with labels such as, "Headaches", "Vomiting", "Cuts" etc., and if you have a lot of medicines, this can certainly be a good idea.

As with everything else in my house, I like to keep medicines to a minimum and so I don't need to have loads of different boxes. I use an old wicker hamper and inside it I have a couple of shoeboxes to divide up the medicines. On one side I have children's medicines, in the middle I have a bag full of plasters and bandages, and on the other side I have the adult medicines. This is all stored on top of a wardrobe so that it is out of reach of them children, and they know not to touch it anyway.

However, because I ~~am a lazy mother and~~ like to encourage autonomy for my children, I like them to be able to access various things without my help. My children are forever falling over and cutting themselves, or running into the nettles, or getting stung by something, so I have a box in the kitchen with plasters, antiseptic cream and bite cream so that they can treat themselves for these, and also so that I can easily grab the box if I'm treating something larger. I also keep the digital thermometer next to it so that it is easily accessible for me if I want to check if they have a fever. I keep saline solution and an eye bath in there which are brilliant for small things in eyes, which seems to happen a lot in this household!

Setting up a First-Aid Kit.

A good First-Aid kit is invaluable for any home. In my kit, I also keep a note of the important numbers and the postcodes for the hospital and doctor's surgery on the inside of the First-Aid tin. In an emergency, sometimes your brain can go blank, so having the numbers accessible like this is helpful.

A Good First-Aid Kit

• Plasters	• Sticky tape
• Small, medium and large gauze	• Thermometer
	• Skin rash cream
• Sterile eye dressing	
	• Insect bite/antihistamine Cream
• Triangular bandage	
• Rolled bandage	• Antiseptic cream
• Safety pins	• Scissors
• Sterile gloves	• Painkillers
• Tweezers	• Distilled water for wounds
• Alcohol-free cleansing wipes	• Saline eye wash and bath

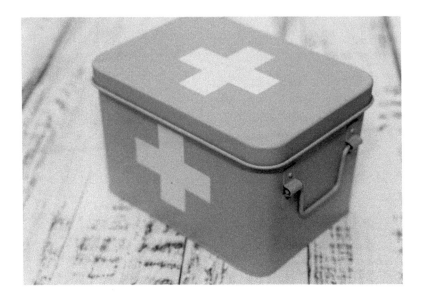

Self-Care Summary

Questions to ask yourself:
• Do I use it?
• How long has it been open?
Tasks to Do:
• Declutter
• Clean Make Up brushes
• Consider simple swaps
• Set up a First Aid kit
Storage
• Travel bottles should go in the travel box
• Keep surfaces clear
• Store Like with Like
• Boxes to corral items

Self-Care Checklist

Make-up	Body
○ Tools/brushes (Wash them!) ○ Eye Makeup ○ Foundation ○ Lips	○ Fake tan ○ Moisturisers ○ Sunscreen
Hair ○ Brushes ○ Accessories ○ Appliances ○ Dye ○ Hair ties etc.	**Nails** ○ Nail varnish ○ Varnish remover ○ Files/Clippers ○ Nail care
Toiletries ○ Shampoo ○ Conditioner ○ Body wash ○ Bubble bath/bombs ○ Soap/hand wash ○ Cotton Wool etc.	**Relaxation** ○ Candles ○ Oils ○ Oil Burners etc.
Teeth ○ Toothbrushes ○ Toothpaste etc.	**Medicine cabinet** ○ Prescription medicine ○ Over the counter medicine ○ Plasters etc.

Bathrooms

A decluttered and well organised bathroom can feel like a Spa and a sanctuary from the world. Often bathrooms can be quite small, so being ruthless with your decluttering and having a strong vision are really helpful here.

Keep surfaces clear for cleaning and designate a space for each member of the household.

Bathroom Worksheet

How do you feel about your bathroom?	Describe your ideal bathroom.
What works?	
What doesn't?	What needs to change?

Chapter 6

Linens

This is a category I really enjoy, although don't talk to my lovely client J about the time I said, "Tell you what, why don't we go for a quick win with the linen cupboard?!" and we crawled out five hours later, on our knees, utterly exhausted, having almost ended up in A&E with an eye injury due to a sewing machine malfunction.

Sheets

Gather together all your sheets, pillow cases, pillows, duvet covers, duvets, blankets, throws and anything else that you might use to make up beds. Remember that there are no short cuts here – yes, this takes effort and time, but you really will reap the rewards in the longer term in the form of an Easy Life.

In linens, I find a lot of, "Just in case". People don't want to let go of the extra pillows or sets of linen in case they need them for guests, or in times of illness. As well as choosing the ones that you love, I have two practical suggestions here. The first is to remember that it is frequently possible to borrow if you need them, or even that people are often happy to bring their own, which is the perfect Easy Life solution. The second is to work out how many beds you have in your house and what is the realistic maximum number that you are likely to need at any one time.

In my house, we have one king-size bed. Then each of the four children have their own single bed and in addition to that, there are four trundle beds and a futon mattress. That is a total of nine single beds that might be made up at any one time, although at least two of those can be made up as a king size instead. Whilst we do frequently have guests, for the majority of the time, it is just us in our home. Many of our duvets are the type that are "multiple season", so ones where you have two duvets that attach together and these can easily be split for guests (in Scotland it has to be said that our guests are more frequent in Summer than in Winter, can't think why...).

To talk numbers, we have two sets of king-sized sheets, each child has two sets of sheets and then there are three spare sets. I'm sure that you can do the maths to see that we have as many as we'll ever need whilst only ever really having a few sitting in the linen cupboard.

For storage, I recommend learning how to fold a fitted sheet (you can see how on my website) and then storing the entire set (duvet cover, sheet, extra pillow cases) inside the pillow case so that it can be easily accessed. I store the sets in the room that they are going to be used in rather than in a specific cupboard, but both storage methods are valid. The point should be that wherever you choose to store them, it is easy for you.

Towels

Gather all of your towels in your home, and including hand towels and tea towels, as well as the larger towels and bathmats. Then stop and have a think about how many towels you actually need. Again, this will change from household to household and will depend on the number of members of the household there are, how often you wash those towels and how quick the turnaround is when you wash them.

If you have lots of towels and you are struggling with which ones to keep, try lining them up in order of preference and then deciding how many you need, and cutting off after that number in the line.

We are a family of six. We wash towels once a week and they are washed and dried on the same day. The children all have a colour coded towel and flannel so that they know which is theirs and my husband and I both hang our towels back on our own pegs, so we don't get them confused either. Therefore, each of us has one bath towel and one flannel. I have two further sets of towels that I keep for guests.

Each family member also has a towel that we take to the swimming pool or beach (kept in the swimming box with the costumes and swimming bags) and finally, we each have a microfibre towel for taking on holiday that is stored in the Travel Box. We have never needed more than this – on the odd occasion that we have more than two guests to stay, we can either bring out the swimming towels, or I can borrow towels from my mother, or the guests might bring them themselves, which again is the perfect Easy Life solution.

Elsewhere in the house, I have a number of scrubby towels that I use for the dogs, cats and horses. These are kept folded in a different basket so that they don't get mixed up with the rest. Bathmats are also washed once a week here, and we only have one bathroom between the 6 of us, which simplifies that matter somewhat.

When you have decided what you are keeping and what is going, it's time to decide what to do with the discards. Good quality spares are often welcomed at refuges and those that are not in such good condition are often greatly in demand in animal rescue centres.

Linen Summary

- Work out how many you need and declutter accordingly

- Remember you can borrow if needed

- Learn how to fold a fitted sheet

- Store sets together in a pillow case

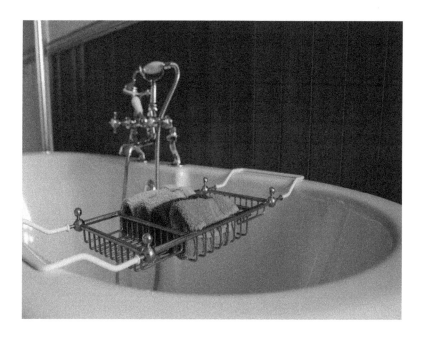

Linen Worksheet

Sheets	Towels
How many beds do you have in your home of each type?	How many people do you have in your household?
How frequently do you change your sheets?	How frequently do you wash your towels and what is the turnaround?
How many sets of sheets do you therefore need?	How many Towels do you therefore need?

Linen Checklist:

Towels	Sheets
○ Large	○ Single
○ Hand	○ Double
○ Kitchen	○ King
○ Bathmats	

Chapter 7

Utility Space

I consider myself extremely fortunate to have a dedicated Utility Room, where my washing machine, tumble dryer and general laundry supplies live. However, it has not always been the case and for many of my clients the items in this utility category live within the kitchen. In spite of this, I have separated these things out into their own chapter as they naturally go together and form a cohesive section distinct from the food theme of the Kitchen

Cleaning

Just like we do for each category, you need to gather all your cleaning supplies in one place. Your cloths, sponges and actual cleaning products. Bring them all together and see what you have. Do you have multiple supplies of some items that you hadn't realised? How are the cloths looking? While I can see that it might be hard to see how you can love cleaning products, it has to be said that a clean home is definitely a positive contribution to your life. It's also easier to convince yourself to clean if you can find the products easily and if you like the things that you are handling.

When we moved into our farmhouse, the previous owners had left some products behind and it took me a year or so to realise that I was never actually going to use these and to let them go. Some were unopened and could go to food banks, whilst others were old and fit only for pouring down the sink with the packaging recycled, and some just had to go in the bin. Sometimes you might realise that you have open duplicates, in which case you can amalgamate them into one container, but please do make sure that they are the same type as some products can react with each other in a very unpleasant fashion.

Once you have gone through your supplies and rationalised them, it's time to think about where to store them. I don't know how everyone else likes to do this, but I certainly find that it's easiest to clean areas if the supplies are handy. My bathroom and downstairs toilet both have a bottle of toilet cleaner and bathroom cleaner in them as I find it easier to just grab them there than to go into the kitchen where the other cleaning supplies are stored. As for the rest of my supplies, I have a tub with a handle that is stored under my sink (it's easy to take around with me), and other supplies are stored in one of those great over-the-door storage racks.

People frequently ask me about how to organise the under the sink area and there is no denying that it can be tricky with pipework. However, like with most of my suggestions, my advice here is simple; the fewer things that you have, the easier it is to keep them organised. I have no fancy solutions under my own sink, but it is tidy and easy to find everything because I keep products to a minimum.

Shoe Cleaning

Don't forget to check your shoe cleaning kit with the rest of your cleaning products. Check that the polishes have not dried out and that the brushes and cloths are still good.

Cleaning Schedules

There are a lot of different schedules out there for cleaning and they are easy to find on the internet. How you clean your home will depend on your personal preference. With so many beings in my home, it is a rare day to find it sparkling. For me, life is too short and I am a great believer that dirt is beneficial to the immune system, so you'll not find me on my hands and knees scrubbing the floor and meticulously dusting behind the radiators.

I tend to move away from too many chemicals, over-scented products and air fresheners – if the house is smelly then I open the windows which is a perfect easy option. I therefore prefer to guide my clients towards systems that minimise time spent cleaning. Much like my attitude to organising, which is "Get it done and move on", so my attitude to cleaning is, "How little time can I spend doing this?".

When it comes to the actual cleaning, I use what I like to term, "The Lazy Mum Method" and that involves getting the rest of the family to do it, because why should it all fall on to my shoulders? I'm not the only resident here, it's the responsibility of all members of the home to keep it clean.

Even when I was at home all day with the children, my first responsibility was to be a mother (and an educator), not a cleaner. As my children have grown, I have taken the time to teach them how to do tasks such as pick up their toys, fold their laundry and put their dishes away in the dishwasher. As they got older, more advanced tasks, such as making their own lunch, dusting, and hoovering were added and we are now at the point where most of the cleaning is done by them.

It undoubtedly took me time to teach them how to do it; initially it would have been much faster to do it myself. They are also not angelic children, they didn't arrive on this earth fully able to wield a cloth and willing to do their share, but I have added tasks step by step, scaffolding them as I go, so that now I am able call out, "Time for Cleaning" and it gets done. It is worth noting that we all clean together at the same time, so that everyone feels part of the team, rather than put upon.

Like many suggestions for living an easy life, it involved an investment of time and energy up-front, but now I can sit back and know that it will be done. I am often asked how I make sure that they clean to my standards and my reply is usually, "My standards are pretty low!", but more seriously, I know that they clean to my standards, because I have taught them to do so. If I come across an area of the home that has not been cleaned properly, I pick them up on it, or alternatively, I just kick back in the happy knowledge that it was not me who had to clean it.

I do not pay my children to do this. Chores and helping in the home are part of being a member of this household. I will, however, pay them if they are doing a task that is allocated as mine. For example, cleaning the kitchen is my job. If I want them to clean it, then I pay them. However, clearing the table or mucking out the stables is everyone's job; these are jobs that just need to be done.

If you live on your own, or with only one other person, then obviously you won't have the luxury of this method, but on the other hand, your house will almost certainly be cleaner than mine anyway as there will be fewer beings in it!

If you are keen to see how I organise my cleaning, then head over to my website to see an example.

Laundry

Into this category come baskets, sorting systems, washing powder, pegs, dryer balls, bags for washing delicates in, ironing boards, ironing board covers and irons. As usual, bring it all to one place, categorise and go through each category and, as always, only you can decide on the right number for you.

I keep types of washing powder to a minimum. My skin reacts quite badly to some detergents so having found one that I can use, I stick to it and wash everything in it, regardless of what it is made of. That might fill some people with horror, but it works for us by keeping the number of supplies to a minimum. We have laundry detergent on a subscription service, so we never run out.

We have two dirty laundry baskets, one in the bathroom, which is downstairs, and one in our bedroom, which is upstairs. I prefer not to have extras in the children's bedrooms because I find then it seems to land on MY shoulders to collect them, whereas if the baskets are in the bathroom, it is the children's responsibility to make sure that their clothes land in them.

Clean laundry baskets: we have one for each family member. As clothes are dried, they go into the relevant basket and then there is no excuse for it not to be sorted. I have invested a significant amount of time teaching my kids how to fold properly, but it's paid so many dividends. The inevitable odd socks stay in the laundry basket until their partner has come through the wash and so they are only put away in pairs.

As for laundry schedules, again, this will depend on your situation, but it really is worth having one so that you know what is washed when, thus removing the need for any conscious thought and reducing the amount of effort that you have to put into this. For example, I wash sheets on Tuesdays and towels on Thursdays, then at least two loads of clothes every other day (except Sunday when I give the washing machine a day off!). If you live on your own, or with just one other person, you'll probably find that you don't need to wash anything like so frequently, but if you have a family, I'd recommend trying to get a load of washing in every day, even if it's just so you don't spend the weekend playing catch up.

Cleaning and Laundry Summary

- It's easier to clean if you like your products
- Get rid of products you don't use
- Keep under the sink organised by decluttering
- Amalgamate duplicates
- Keep them where you clean (or at least a subset)
- Unless you live on your own, cleaning the home is not solely your responsibility
- Set up a cleaning rota
- Have a clean laundry basket for each family member
- Create a laundry schedule
- Teach family members to fold their own clothes
- Keep odd socks in baskets until the pair is found

Cleaning Rota

To make a cleaning rota of your own, write down the tasks that need to be done on a Daily, Weekly, Monthly and less frequent basis and allocate them to a time.

Daily	Weekly	Monthly	Less

Use the chart below make a laundry schedule, taking into account activities that go on during the week.

Day	Laundry
Monday	
Tuesday	
Wednesday	
Thursday	
Friday	
Saturday	
Sunday	

Utility Room

A separate utility room is a real boon, but these rooms can end up being dumping grounds. Try to prevent this with a clear vision of how you would like this room to function. If you don't have a separate room, then designate part of your home (possibly a station in the kitchen, or a cupboard in a hallway) as an area where you store these items together.

Utility Checklist

Cleaning Supplies	Laundry Supplies
o Washing up	o Detergent
o Bathroom	o Conditioner
o Kitchen	o Dryer sheets/Balls
o Other	o Baskets
o Hoover	o Iron
o Broom and pan	o Ironing board
o Other Electrical	
o Shoe Cleaning	

Utility Worksheet

How do you feel about your utility?	Describe your ideal utility.
What works?	
What doesn't?	What needs to change?

Pets

I'm guessing that most people don't have quite as many pets as we do, but it is easy to rack up many belongings for our precious animals regardless of how many pets you have.

As always, gather all of the pet related items from wherever they are spread around your home and bring them together into one place. Subcategorise as necessary and then see how many of each you have. Make sure that you have an appropriate number of each item and that any old medicines or flea treatments that are past their use-by date are discarded. Put aside anything that needs mending and make sure that it gets done.

How many of each item you will decide to keep will always be entirely up to you and your particular circumstances. For me, I prefer having fewer items because it means that I can keep them tidy more easily. I will admit that pets themselves are an area where I lean towards excess but they bring me so much joy! For other people it might be clothes, or handbags, or craft materials, for me it is animals.

Chapter 8

Kitchen

Without further ado, let's get on to our kitchens. Kitchens are divided into four main areas for decluttering: the food we eat, the utensils that we cook with, the implements that we eat with and miscellaneous items. Let's start with food.

Food

I hate food waste. Such a poor use of precious resources. To prevent it in my own home, I regularly go through the food in both my fridge and my cupboards.

To do a food declutter, pull all the food out. I recommend doing it in categories such as fresh, frozen and ambient.

First, go through it all and look for expiry dates and discard those that are past it. There are two types of expiry dates. Use By should NOT be used beyond the date, whilst Best Before can often be used, but just won't taste as good. However, if you haven't eaten tinned or packaged food by the expiry date, that it is unlikely that you are going to and you should go ahead and get rid of it. In the future, make sure that you don't buy it again, or (if it is half used), try and buy a smaller amount.

Once you have date checked and discarded the easy wins, take a look at your food in the fridge and check for how long it can be used after it has been opened. I take many of the lengths with a pinch of salt, but if it says that it should be eaten within 10 days and it is 6 months later, do yourself a favour and get rid of it. If it is something you don't use frequently, use a permanent marker to label when you open the jar in the future so that you know how long it has been open for.

Take a long hard look at the rest of the food that is within date, and decide if it is something that you are going to use. Sometimes we buy things because they seem like a good idea, but the reality is that we simply don't use them. Sometimes we may have been gifted an item that we won't use. If the items are unopened and in date, then take them to a food bank - your local supermarket will usually have one.

If the food packets are opened, but within date and you will not use them, then see if any of your friends or family might like them (but do not take them to them without prior permission, that is just passing on the problem to someone else). If it is food that is opened and that is within date, but that you cannot rehome, then go ahead and put it in the food waste and try to take a lesson from it and not buy it again. Do not just put it back in the cupboard until it's out of date. That is a waste of your time, energy and space.

Take this time whilst your food is out of its usual place to give the cupboards or fridge a good wipe down and clean. When it comes to putting the food back in the cupboards, store like with like to make it easier to find things.

If you have children and they have things that they help themselves to, try to make sure that these things are within reach to foster independence, remembering that in reach for a child is different to in reach for an adult. I am more than happy to put things low down in an awkward cupboard for them because they are more bendy than me!

In my fridge, I have a Lunch Tray, which is a fridge box containing the sort of things that they put in their sandwiches. Corralling it together keeps the fridge tidier and helps them to find what they need and put it away in the correct spot. Their snacks are in a cupboard which is low down and awkward for me to access on a regular basis, but my children are quite happy to rootle through looking for snacks. I don't over categorise the snacks for them either. There's a box of savoury snacks, and a box of sweet snacks. Once a week, when we do the groceries, I check through the box, taking out anything that should no longer be in there (usually empty wrappers) and refill it. Not for me the pantries full of labelled snack boxes – that sounds far too much like hard work!

I am, however, a great fan of decanting pantry supplies. Not things like breakfast cereal (which my kids go through so fast that there's not much point), but things like flour and pasta. I like the way it looks and it helps me to keep on top of what is in the cupboard and what is not. Importantly, it also keeps food fresh and pest free. I store the back-ups in another cupboard and know that when I have taken the last back-up out of the cupboard to be decanted, that it is time to put it on the shopping list again.

It is important to make sure that the food is date rotated. The easiest way to do this is simply to make sure that you don't overstock. When you do have several of one type of product, put new ones at the back and the older ones that should be used sooner will automatically be pushed towards the front.

Fridge Organisation

Whilst the rainbow fridges of Instagram and TikTok are very beautiful, I don't think that they are very realistic for most people. Certainly, whilst my own fridge is organised, it is not rainbowed. I use zones and fridge caddies to maximise space and keep it in order.

On the top shelf, I keep dairy and yogurt. On the next shelf down, leftovers, washed fruit and cans of drinks. The next has the children's lunch tray and the hundreds of apples that they seem to eat. The bottom shelf has the fresh meat, stored in a fridge box to makes sure that no juices leak out, and the open tins of dog and cat food. In the door are the jars and condiments and the milk. Fresh fruit and vegetables are stored in the chiller drawers. Even a fairly simple organisational structure like this means that it is easy to find things and to see when we are likely to need to replenish stocks.

Freezer Organisation

In my freezer, on the top shelf are the desserts, then the batch cooked meals (because why cook a meal twice when you can do it once and freeze a portion?). The bottom shelf is full of frozen veggies and chips, whilst the frozen meat is in the drawers. We use a board marker to label the tubs before they go in and we use stickies on the front of the freezer to let us know what is in there, to avoid things being forgotten.

Because we live in deepest darkest rural Scotland, it is not unusual for us to get snowed in during the winter, so I like to have a bit of back-up stock in the cupboards and also in the deep freeze. Our deep freeze has the same sticky note system on it to prevent things from getting lost in there.

Cooking Utensils

Once you've got your food safely packed away again, it's time to try the utensils. If you feel like that would be overwhelming, you can break it down into smaller categories: for example saucepans, frying pans, implements, knives, cake tins, small electrical appliances like toasters, slow cookers etc. but again, do ensure that you find EVERYTHING in that category (and wipe down the shelves as you remove things).

Take a good look at each category and only keep the items that you honestly use, ensuring that you handle each item. Remember that you can usually borrow items from friends and family if you suddenly find yourself feeding the five thousand.

The finished result will look different for everyone. In my household, we're a larger family and we cook almost every meal from scratch, so we have quite a lot of equipment; particularly things for baking, which is something that my husband really enjoys doing. I would be happier with a fraction of the tins and trays that he has, but he loves them, so they stay. He would be happier with fewer animals in the home, but I love those, so they stay – it's all a matter of balance.

However, that's not to say that we're overwhelmed with equipment. For example, we get by very easily with 3 saucepans, two frying pans and a wok. I use my trusty casserole dish for so many things and I long ago got rid of things that we don't use like the slow cooker. We don't have much electrical equipment as we have one (ok, two), of those fancy super-duper machines that does everything – food processes, chops, cooks, steams and washes itself up. It's the ideal lazy person's tool and takes up less space than the number of things that it replaces, which means that my kitchen is emptier and therefore easier to use. Take a look at the number of appliances that you have for cooking and ask yourself if they are truly making your life easier, or are they just taking up space?

Dinnerware

Time to define and gather categories again! For example, cutlery, serving utensils, serving dishes, crockery, glasses, mugs and so on. Do remember that there is no predefined or set number of items for you to keep, you must keep the right number of items for you and your situation. Some items will be easy to make decisions on: there will be some that you love and some that you will wonder why you even had it in your home.

For other things though, it might be a bit harder for you to decide, so here are a couple of questions that you might find useful.

"How many of these do I use on a regular basis?" and "Could I borrow this item if I needed it?"

Do remember to use the good stuff every day, the perfect time is now. It's so sad to find sets in the cupboard that no one will ever use. Use the beautiful plates and delightful glasses, don't leave them to gather dust in the cupboard. Yes, over time some will get broken, but how much worse for them to never leave the cupboard, or only on special occasions? We use ours on a daily basis. It's also worth remembering that tastes change between generations. What one generation thinks is fabulous, the next will think is dated. Don't hang on to your best china thinking that your children or grandchildren will love it - they probably won't and they may well just toss it out. So use it!

Miscellaneous Kitchen

Finally in the kitchen is the miscellaneous category, the odds and ends.

Check your handtowels, tea towels, table cloths and napkins. We have three handtowels that are changed regularly (somehow, they get much dirtier than the ones in the bathroom!) and a few tea towels that bring me joy, mainly because of the memories associated with buying them. I get rid of any that are tatty. With tablecloths and napkins, if you have a number of them, ask yourself if you use them and which ones you reach for, then release the rest.

An area that many people struggle with in the kitchen is food storage solutions. By this I mean what we decant supplies into and the storage of batch cooked meals or leftovers. Some people like glass, some people like plastics, some people like bags. In this area, like in so many others, the answer to keeping it tidy is to declutter, declutter, declutter. Be honest with yourself about the number of containers

that you will use. Unlike much of the rest of the kitchen supplies, which are used, washed and returned to their home, storage solutions should be in use. As a general rule, the container cupboard should be normally pretty empty because the items are in use. If it is constantly overflowing, then you simply have too many. I stick to one brand /type of tub in just a few sizes. I like the way that they all stack inside and on top of one another, and if a tub or a lid gets broken, then there are replacements.

Lunch boxes are another area where people struggle to keep organised and the advice is the same. Declutter as much as you are able, and stick to one type or system to make storage easier.

Don't forget any wraps that you have for keeping food fresh, be they wax, foil or plastic. This is also an easy place to make sustainable swaps – swapping out single use plastics for multi-use wraps.

Layout and Storage

When you have finished with deciding what you want to keep, now is the time to look at overall kitchen storage. Every kitchen is different in layout of course, but here are some general recommendations.

As far as possible, I recommend that you keep your kitchen surfaces clear. The clearer they are, the easier they are to keep clean, and the easier they are to keep clean, the nicer the cooking experience is. I keep only the very frequently used items on my kitchen surface and I avoid using things like knife blocks, which clutter up the area.

When deciding where to put things, the areas within easy reach are absolutely prime storage, so the lower shelves of upper cabinets and the upper areas in the lower cabinets. Put the things that you use most often in these areas, assigning items that you use less frequently to the areas that are more difficult to reach. Take into account the different heights of the household members - I mentioned earlier in this chapter that I put my children's snacks in a cupboard that is low down because they are more than happy to scramble round in cabinets that are inconvenient for me. The same goes for my husband; he is considerably taller than me, so I can put things that he uses frequently and that I don't (such as the healthy snack tub!) on a higher shelf.

Store like with like - it is useful to create stations or areas. I keep all my drinks near the glasses (a cocktail station can be fun to set up if this is your thing!), my tea and coffee near the kettle. I have an area that is put to one side for food prep. I like to store the plates and bowls next to the dishwasher and sink which makes it easier to put them away. I keep my sharp knives in a drawer separate from my other utensils to prevent accidents with my children. A lunch box station if you have children (or adults!) for making packed lunches is extremely helpful.

Heavy items should be stored close to the bottom. Not only will this prevent them from breaking shelves, but it will save your back as it is easier to lift them from there. Lighter items, including glassware,

can be stored higher up and this looks nicer as well as being easier.

Look for vertical storage solutions, such as hooks under cabinets for cups, vertical risers in cupboards and don't forget that you can put storage on the inside of doors if the door is strong enough to take it. I use racks to store baking trays vertically which helps when accessing them as you don't have to dig around underneath. In awkward shaped cupboards where it is difficult to see the items, I use turntables so that I can bring all the products easily to the front.

If you are lucky enough to design a new kitchen from scratch, I cannot recommend pan drawers enough. Having a drawer that slides out, so that it is easy to reach the items stored at the back, is wonderfully convenient. However, if, like me, you are stuck with cupboards on the bottom, do not despair! I use boxes in some of these cupboards that I can use like drawers and pull out.

If you are designing a kitchen from scratch, do look for cupboards that go all the way to the ceiling and also that have kick drawers all the way down at the bottom.

Kitchen Summary

- Discard out of date food
- Buy smaller packets if necessary
- Keep a permanent marker to mark when a packet is opened
- Use the good stuff every day!
- If your "Tupperware" is over flowing, you have too much
- Stick to one type of storage container

Questions to consider:

- If it broke would I replace it?
- How often would I need this?
- Could I borrow it if I needed to?

Things to consider when storing:

- Store like with like
- Make Stations
- Make use of Prime space
- Consider heights of users
- Store heavy at the bottom, light at the top
- Use vertical space:
  - Shelf Risers
  - Shelf Steps
  - Vertical holders
  - Back of door storage

Kitchen Worksheet

What currently works in your kitchen?	Describe your ideal kitchen
What doesn't work?	

Draw a plan of your kitchen, marking out the sink (and dishwasher if you have one), fridge and cooker.

Kitchen Storage Worksheet

Where are your prime spaces?	Where can you place vertical storage?
Which items need to be in the prime spaces?	What storage solutions would make your life easier?
Which items do you use less frequently (and can be put in the less accessible space)?	
What "Stations" would be useful in your kitchen?	

Kitchen Checklist

Food
- Carbohydrates
- Dry goods
- Canned Goods
- Jams/Spreads
- Snacks
- Drinks
  (incl. tea/coffee)
- Fridge
- Freezer

Cooking
- Pots and pans
- Baking trays and dishes
- Cake tins
- Utensils
  - Ladles
  - Spatulas
  - Knives

Small Appliances

Crockery
- Plates
- Bowls
- Serving dishes
- Cutlery

Drinkware
- Mugs
- Glasses
- Travel Mugs

Disposable
- Tissues
- Foil, cling film etc.
- Kitchen Roll
- Wraps
- Lunch boxes
- Disposable bags
- Shopping bags

Tableware
- Tablecloths
- Placemats
- Napkins
- Coasters

Menu Planning

Why Menu Plan? We menu plan so that we have don't have the soul-destroying task of trying to decide what to feed the children every evening. It also makes grocery shopping easy and fast and reduces the likelihood of food waste. Knowing that we have the ingredients in to cook dinner means that we're less likely to order a takeaway or end up having beans on toast. It also means that we can make sure that we eat a variety of food.

The easiest way to menu plan is to start by brainstorming all the meals that you enjoy. Once you have a list, put them into rough categories such as beef, pasta, curry, and see if you can work them into a rolling menu.

We have a 4-week rolling menu that is based upon the following:

Monday: Stir Fry.

Tuesday: Fish or pork (steamed, poached, in a pie, sausages),

Wednesday: Beef (including Bolognese, meatballs).

Thursday: Chicken (with pasta, potatoes, rice, whatever!)

Friday: Fish and chips for the kids, a more sophisticated meal for the adults.

Saturday: Pizza for Movie night!

Sunday: Roast.

We make sure that things are spread out so that we don't have Lasagne and Chicken Alfredo in the same week, that the Pork in Hoisin Sauce (stir fry) is not in the same week as Toad in the Hole. Meals fall in and out of fashion in our house too. For years, we enjoyed Chicken and Boursin pie, then the kids hated it, now they love it.

We don't stick rigidly to it. We check diaries when we plan and will shift things around depending on the activities we are doing. Some days we get home exhausted and say, "How about we just have Scrambled Eggs?", or maybe we've been out and had a sneaky takeaway on our way home. In which case, we'll look at the menu, see what can be moved around, what can be easily frozen and go from there. But the crux of the matter is that we know that there is food we can cook at home and that all the ingredients are there. It takes the mental effort out of feeding the family.

The excess from our dinners tends to go in the freezer, to either eat as a lunch, or because we have deliberately cooked as a batch and it means that next time we want to eat Bolognese, we know that there is a portion already in the freezer and it makes things super easy.

Groceries

We try to shop for groceries just once a week with a planned menu and list as it reduces impulse buying (which helps with budgeting too). We have a list of store cupboard basics that we can refer to, but probably our strongest asset, other than meal planning, is a shopping list app that we share as a family. If anyone opens the last of an item, they simply open the app, tap on the item and it goes on the shopping list.

Menu Planning Worksheet

Make a list of meals that your household enjoys	Make a list of essentials for your store cupboard:

Plan next week's menu (check your diary!):

	Breakfast	Lunch	Dinner	Snack
Monday				
Tuesday				
Wednesday				
Thursday				
Friday				
Saturday				
Sunday				

Don't forget to write a list before going shopping!

Chapter 9

Books

Books are an emotive category for many people but remember, just like in every other category that we cover, there is no right or wrong number of books that you should keep. I read fiction mainly on my e-reader, but I like to have reference books in physical form. I do have some of my favourite fiction in physical form and when I was writing this I went to have a little count of how many books we have on our shelves. I have about thirty physical fiction books and about double the number of reference books. Mr Tidy Coo has about seventy, and my children have about seven hundred. As long as you handle every single book in your collection, then keep as many as you would like.

I'm an absolute bookworm; I love to read and will often read over 100 books a year. However, there is no denying that physical books take up a lot of space and once a book is read, it's usually placed on the shelf never to be read again. It is not unusual for me to go into people's homes and find piles of books that haven't been read but which are piling up in corners. Some people buy books seeking the excitement of owning something new and the momentary euphoria that comes with that, but then rarely read all these books that they have bought.

The time to read a book is when it first enters your home. Piles of unread books cause overwhelm and can decrease the amount of time you spend reading. Often people find that when they release their enormous pile of unread books, they actually read more. Therefore, even as someone who loves books, I would encourage you to audit your collection, however small or large.

Historically, books have been incredibly hard to get hold of. Initially produced and copied by monks, they conferred social status and were held in a sacred regard. Even in more recent times, books were still expensive – something that you saved up for and certainly not something that you discarded when you were finished. As almost the only way to pass information between generations, they were, rightly, venerated. Now, we live in the Information Age with access to everything at our fingertips on the internet, and yet there is still a cultural panic at the thought of letting books go - almost as if by letting the book go, you let the knowledge, or the fact that you read it, go. Some people like to keep books as if they were trophies.

The books you read only contribute to who you are, they do not define you. They are not your memories and releasing the book does not mean that the knowledge you gained will suddenly dissipate. It is also worth remembering that even Libraries let go of books and publishers will regularly pulp books when they have too many. Remember that someone will eventually be tasked with discarding your books and, if they are important to you, make sure that you have done most of the hard work for them.

The key to this category, as with every category, is to handle everything. The books need to come off your shelves in order to be properly checked. I like to tell the story of a client, who said to me that she was categorically keeping every book about horses. Now, with 8 ponies of my own, I completely understood that, but I persuaded her to check them anyway. We did, and whilst she kept most of the books on horses, she released about a fifth of them, including one book that actually made her so angry that she burned it! No one needs that kind of negative energy on their shelves, so do handle all of them, and that means taking them off the shelves to do so.

As you start the audit of your shelves, I want you to make sure that you have pen and paper with you, or some other way to make notes. That way, if you come across an unread book that you are afraid to let go, you can write down the title so that you remember it. In the unlikely event that you suddenly decide that you want to read it, you will be able to easily refer back to it.

Similarly, in the future, when you are given an excellent reading suggestion from someone, rather than buy it immediately, make a note of the title and, when you next come to need a book, scan the list of titles and see which one you feel like reading.

Things to consider when you are decluttering books

Be wary of dust! Books that are stored on shelves tend to get very dusty. Make sure that you have some sort of dusting equipment with you, such as a Dustbuster, or a damp cloth.

Be careful handling large numbers of books and climbing up to get them. Make sure that if you are clambering around to reach the higher shelves, that you have something secure to stand on and that you don't make yourself ache by moving large numbers at once. It may well be worth clearing space on a table rather than putting them on the floor as this will help to protect your back.

Check each book before you discard it as sometimes small documents may be wedged in it.

Initially, don't worry about what you are going to do with the discards; just focus on what you are keeping - and don't get caught up in reading books, or this will take you forever! How does each book make you feel? What feeling or emotion will it be enhancing if it stays on your shelves? If you pick up a book and feel nothing from picking it up, then it's unlikely that it is worth it staying on your shelves. The books that I love, that I have here, make me smile.

How long have you owned it? If you have had a book in your possession for a length of time and it remains unread, then you are unlikely to read it. Opinions on this time period differ, some say more than a month and others more than 6 months. Ask yourself why you are still keeping it. You can make a small pile of books that you would really love to read still, but be wary of making it too large or it will start to overwhelm you. One strategy to use with these books that you are really keen to read, is to put a moratorium on buying any more until you have read them (remember, you can make a note of the titles instead), and if that thought makes you cringe, then it's time to be honest with yourself and admit that these books are only gathering dust.

Has it fulfilled its purpose? Will you read it or refer to it again? If you're unlikely to do so, then don't let it gather dust on your shelves, release it so that someone else can.

Are the contents current? This is an important question, particularly with travel or textbooks, which often seem to go out of date as soon as they are written.

How hard would it be to find again? Usually it's pretty easy to pick a book up if you suddenly have an overwhelming desire to read it, but sometimes a book may be a one off, or a special or signed edition, in which case, if you are uncertain, it may be worth keeping.

Is it worth the real estate? How much space are you willing to give over to the storage of books? I've had clients who had lost entire rooms to books. Rooms that they would prefer to use for something else, such as a spare bedroom, or an office. Would it be better to just have a couple of bookcases worth? Or even just a couple of shelves worth?

Do your books reflect who you are right now, or who you were in the past? It took me a long time to let go of the books that I bought for my degree in Genetics. Massive tomes with names like Gene V. Just like I said at the beginning of this section, I was afraid that by letting them go, I would be letting go of the fact that I had done a degree in Genetics all those years ago. However, I moved out of that field a long time ago and the information in it was no doubt very out of date by the time I let it go, so I gave myself permission to stop dragging it around. I've still got my degree, but having moved on, first to teaching, and then to Professional Organising, there really was no need at all for me to keep the book, no matter how much it cost me as a penniless student.

Who are you keeping it for? Sometimes clients tell me that they are keeping a particular book for their children, but do bear in mind that they may well not want it! Don't burden other people with decisions that you can't make yourself.

How you organise your books is, of course, totally up to you, and if you want to rainbow them, you go right ahead. However, I would suggest that you organise by topic and author so that you can begin to see overlaps.

What to do with the discards?

There are excellent apps where you scan barcodes and get a buying price which is a good way to get rid of books and feel like you've made something from the sale. There are also Charities that will come and collect books and hand them on to people who need them. Most Charity shops will take book donations and it's always worth asking your local library, homeless shelter and or hospital if they would take them.

My friends and I pass books on a lot between ourselves – I have a shelf of books in my home that people are welcome to browse and to take from and there are communities where people have set up tiny libraries, which strikes me as an excellent idea. It is worth remembering that even recycling them is sending them on to their next useful life.

Books Summary

- Only you know the right number for you
- Books contribute towards you, they do not define you
- Physical Books take up a lot of space
- The time to read a book is when it enters your home
- Unread books create overwhelm
- Releasing them often increases the amount of time spent reading
- Sooner or later, someone will have to deal with your books
- Handle everything
- Use a notebook
- Be wary of dust
- Take care of your back
- Check for small documents
- Hold and feel rather than re-read

Questions to ask yourself:

- How does it make you feel?
- How long have you owned it?
- Has it fulfilled its purpose?
- Are the contents current?
- Would it be hard to find again?
- Is it worth the Real Estate?
- Who are you keeping it for?
- Does it reflect who you are now?

Future Books

- Make a note of titles.
- Why are you buying the book?
- When will you read it?
- Make use of the library.
- Could you get it digitally?

Books Checklist

- ○ Fiction
- ○ Text/Reference
- ○ Travel
- ○ Cookery
- ○ Coffee table
- ○ Magazines

Chapter 10

Living Area

We covered the categories that I generally expect to find in the bedroom, bathroom, utility and kitchen, so now we are on to categories I expect to find in the living area. Even if you don't store these categories in your living spaces, go through this chapter and check which of them you do have in your home and make sure to do them!

Music and Videos

For me, the flip side of Books is Music and Video. Whilst some people have thousands of books, others prefer to watch or listen instead and may have many CDs, DVDs, cassettes, VHS, vinyl, and even cinefilm.

Solid forms for music are a funny one as depending on when you were born, you may have thousands of items, or you may have none at all. One of the things that I often find in people's houses is that they have media that they are unable to play – particularly cassettes. Anything that is on a tape has a limited length of time that it can be played for as the tape degrades, and often quite quickly. If you have something that is on a tape of any type and you want to keep it, you need to consider getting it converted to digital.

For the declutter itself, gather all of your music, film and TV collection together and sort it into categories by type. In this situation, I am not talking about formats, but genres. With media constantly being superseded by newer formats, you may find that you have several copies of a particular album, or film, so it is worth referencing your digital collections at the same time as doing your physical collection.

When it comes to storage, one way that you can prevent your CDs and DVDs from taking up too much space is to take them out of their cases and put them into a specialist storage bag. You'll have to work out yourself whether or not this is the right solution for you. I don't have any CDs at all, they all belong to my husband as he's the one who is interested in music, so this isn't a category in the house that I have any control over. He didn't want to take his CDs out of their cases as he likes the artwork, so they live in a drawer in the sitting room for him to easily access. DVDs are the same in our home as they don't belong to me. We have found a little nook for them to live in.

Make some playlists that really make you smile and make sure that you are able to easily access the tracks that you love.

Like books, there are places where it is easy to sell the items that you decide to release. Often they'll come with an app that allows you to scan a barcode. I know of at least one person who takes old CDs and makes jewellery out of them. Do check out the sustainability section on my website for links to some of these services.

Board Games/Card games

Continuing with the things that we might find in the living room, I'm going to add board games. Things like Monopoly, Scrabble and playing cards. Bring them all together – put aside those that you don't enjoy playing, and then neatly file the ones that you do, checking for missing pieces as you do. Remember that you can often source replacement pieces for games online. The key is to have the games accessible to encourage playing. I like to leave them in their boxes, but I know many people who decant into folders with zips.

Discards can go to charity shops, or you can try residential care homes.

Home Office

There are not many people who are lucky enough to have a dedicated Home Office space, but it is important to carve out a space within your home where you know that you can access all the things that you might need for whatever you may do in this space. Even if you don't have or need a dedicated space, make sure that you do these categories.

The first step in this of course is to gather together all of your office supplies. Anything that you use to write with, or on, or in or use to keep stuff together and ordered. Pens, pencils, staplers, hole punches, files, notebooks and blank paper. Paperwork itself is a different category that we will tackle later and is defined as anything that is written down and meant to be read.

Once you have ferreted it all out, categorise it and then work through seeing what you actively want to keep. Have a look at the pens that you grab to write with for example – most of us have a favourite type that we would reach for over the others. I would particularly encourage you to check felt tips, coloured pencils and crayons at this point as they have a real tendency to build up.

I often come across large numbers of beautiful, but unused, notebooks in people's homes. They have seen this notebook in a shop, bought it because it is beautiful and then been too afraid to use it for fear of "spoiling" it. Just like we should use the nice tableware and wear the nice clothes every day, so we should use the nice notebooks. Yes, it may get spoilt, but better surely to use them as they were intended than to leave them ignored on a shelf. Either donate or use, and put a moratorium on buying any more until the ones that you have are used, as we did with books.

Once you have decided what you like the best and what you want to keep, it is time to thank the other things and let them go. Many schools are often grateful for stationery that you don't want and there are various recycling schemes that you can access too, both local and nationwide.

There are so many different ways to store office supplies! As a general rule, it can be useful to use smaller boxes within a larger space to help corral like with like and I often hang on to smaller boxes that I pick up along the way (shoe boxes, but also iPhone boxes, chocolate boxes) to help clients when it comes to storage. Try to have a space where you keep it all together and where you know that it can be returned to. But, and this is a big "but", once again, don't break your heart over storage at this point. Remember that during a big declutter of your home, things move around and spaces open up. Use what you already have for now and don't spend your money buying storage solutions until you've worked through all the categories in your home.

If, like most people, you do not have a whole room that you can dedicate to office equipment, it still needs a designated space to be stored.

The final place that you end up storing your things will probably change as you work your way through your home, but it really can be worth creating a Home Command Centre. I know that so many books on organising mention this, but the reason that they do (just like they mention handbag stations or landing strips) is that these systems work.

You can carve out a tiny spot and make it somewhere that you can work in peace. During the 2020 pandemic, when suddenly both my husband and I were working from home, I emptied my linen cupboard (and rehomed the contents throughout my house), put in a couple of shelves at the right height for me and made a tiny office. It was about 60cm wide – just wide enough for a chair, but it was wide enough for me to successfully work! Look for a small underused space.

Crafting

Indoor hobbies and crafts is basically anything that you do indoors that requires various small equipment. So, paper cutting, crochet, sewing, quilting, knitting, origami, drawing, painting – I am sure that there are many that I've missed off!

Much like the Books category, Craft is an area that I often get a lot of push back on. People can get very invested in their yarn collections, or their material collections. There is generally a lot of, "Oh no, I can't possibly let go of any of it, I love it all".

I. Get. This.

However, I want to remind you that in order to have an Easy Life, in order to be able to have the time to do all of the things that you want to be able to do and still not be stressed, then you really must handle everything. Remember the story of my client who burnt a book that she discovered? So it is with Crafting. I'm not asking you to throw away your entire collection, simply to look at it truthfully and see if it is stuff that you would still choose to use.

I used to do a heap of craft myself. I sewed, I quilted, I crocheted, I cross-stitched, I drew. I loved to make things and I had the typical stash of many crafters. However, as time went on and I became busier with children and animals, my crafting fell by the wayside. But my stash still sat there, making faces at me. Sticking its tongue out at me as I walked past it. My rainbow of yarns, my beautiful fabrics. It just all made me feel a bit useless and guilty to be honest. So I decided to do an audit and I have to admit that initially very few things went; I hung on to a lot because I was afraid to let it go.

In spite of this, having spent so much of my time now choosing to live with only stuff that supported me, I went through it again a while later and this time only kept the stuff that I really loved. Only the things that made my heart sing. My stash is now a fraction of the size that it was. I do still have a few pieces. The cross-stitch sampler is now something that I am aiming to finish for my first grandchild (whenever that might be!) because I loved it so much. My owl fabric got made into bags (I had been saving it for something "special" so it had never been used; a classic mistake).

I still have my sewing machine and sewing kit. I still have my lovely wooden crochet hooks (because one day I will use them again!), but I don't have stacks and stacks of stuff that weighs me down. If I have a project that I want to do, I go and buy the materials for it and I do it. I have created an abundance mentality around crafts – the projects that I need to do will come to me when I need to do them.

However, I am aware that there are two types of crafter out there. There is the type that I have become – the "I want to make this, so I shall go and buy the things to make it with" and there is the type that my mother is which is the, "I shall buy this because I love it and then when I want to make something, I will look in my stash and see what I fancy doing" and both ways of doing it are totally valid!

My mother came into her own in late October one year when the kids were small: I rocked up at her house weeping that I was a failure as a Mummy because I had not got Halloween costumes for the children – I'd left it too late to order any, didn't have the energy to make them myself and couldn't face the plastic tat in the shops. My mother rootled through her stash and her dressing up box and delivered four outfits to me the next day, just in time for the Halloween Party. So I am NOT saying that you have to do it the way I am doing it, but I will say that even my mother has been through her material stash and has rationalised it so that she is better able to work with it. She's released the things that she won't use and has only kept the bits that she will. Even if you can't bear to part with any of it, doing an audit of it will be helpful for you so that you can see what you have. If you start to do this audit and feel overwhelmed that you can't, because there is too much of it, then I am going to gently suggest that you focus on the bits that you love and discard the rest.

Often, as is the case with books when having fewer frequently leads to MORE reading, having fewer items in your craft stash actually leads to more creativity. This is certainly the case for children's craft as well.

Once you come to organising it, there are countless ways as usual! Making sure that you can see it all at a glance when you open your storage is important, so file folding material can be useful and vertically storing, like we do with clothing, is super helpful.

Small Electricals

By small electricals I mean everything smaller than a dishwasher that has an electrical component to it. Which includes, but is not limited to, phones (mobile and landline, old and new), laptops and computers, printers, tape/disc players, television sets, broadband routers (you'd be amazed at how many of these I find stashed away), lamps, clocks, microwaves, juicers, and anything else that is powered by electricity or batteries and that we haven't already covered.

As you can see, this is potentially quite a big category and as usual, everyone's number will be different – we have only one TV in the house for example, but we have four iPads (one each for the kids). Do ask yourself, in this ever-changing technological world that we live in, if you have the right number for you.

You know the drill: find everything in the category, bring it together, make positive decisions about what you want to keep and thank the rest before letting it go to the appropriate place.

Remember to make positive choices to keep things rather than hanging on to things "just because". We no longer have a landline or fixed broadband (the speed in rural Aberdeenshire can be shockingly low), but we do have two 4G routers – one for the house and one for my office. Without these 4G units, neither my husband or I would be able to work from home. The one in the house is a bit beefier and we have unlimited data as my kids use it as well, whilst the one in my office has a lower limit and is more portable. Fully charged, I can use it as a mobile hotspot anywhere there is signal, and I can even take it overseas.

As an aside, although it may have been cheaper to roll all the networks in to one, we have chosen to have them on different networks and we've done this as a bit of disaster planning. Whilst a rare occurrence, mobile networks can go down, and if we're all on that network, then we're stuffed! However, being on different networks means that if one does goes down, the other is usually still available.

It is rare to find a donation point for old electricals (most charity shops won't take them), but it is often possible to sell them. Most council operated recycling centres have an electrical recycling area and some manufacturers and retailers will take back and recycle your old devices. Do make sure that you wipe your data from them though and reset the factory settings, as you don't want your digital inform- ation ending up in the wrong hands.

Cables and wires, in particular, seem to breed. Almost every time a new electrical item comes into the house, it brings with it a prolifer- ation of wires and plugs, many for functions you don't need or won't use and for countries you won't visit. When the electrical item is replaced with a new one, the item itself may go to recycling, but the wires seem to stay. So off you go on a wire hunt: collect the unused ones from all over the house and bring them back into a pile.

Categorise them by type and look to see how many you have. First check for any obviously broken ones. Then check if you know what they are for - if not, I suggest you let them go! For the rest, ask yourself if you will actually need that many of each type in your life (particularly Ethernet cables), because the honest reality is that you really won't. Perhaps keep one spare for the instance that the one in use stops working. Otherwise, just let the poor wires go. They can go to small electrical recycling and be recycled and the bits of them used. Far better than sitting in your drawers! Those that are kept, label clearly, wrap up so that they don't tangle everything else, and put in a safe place where you know where to find them.

Decorative Items and Furniture

Often the decor in our house is such that we actually start to ignore it. I would like you to go back to what we did at the start of this book and recall your vision of what you would like your home to look like.

For each of the following categories, ask whether or not you can see this particular item in your vision. Gather categories together and take them out of their usual place if you can, because sometimes taking something out of its usual spot can be a real turning point. What might seem sweet in one spot can lose its appeal when dragged out into the cold light of day in another.

Wall Art

I'm not going to ask you to take every picture off the wall, but I am going to ask you to go and stand in front of each picture and take a long hard look at it. If it is easy to move, I'd suggest that you do take it down and handle it, but if it is a larger one, assess it in place. Do you still love it? Can you remember the feeling it evoked when you bought it? Do you still get that feeling?

If you have a stack of pictures that aren't hung, ask yourself why they aren't. What is stopping you from getting them up on the walls? If you want to put them up, make a note of the next steps that you need to take in order to do so, be it get a tape measure out, or research what type of fixing they need, or where they should go. Do the same as we did with books: a moratorium on new art until the art you already have is appropriately displayed.

Cushions and Throws

Why do you have them? Do they add to your home? Do they just get in the way? Remember the golden rules of handle everything and choose positively. Also remember that when you are making the decision about what to keep, don't worry about what you are going to do with the discards, just worry about whether you love it enough to keep it in your home. Once you have made the decision, then you can worry about how to get it out of your home.

Ornaments

Some of these will be sentimental, some will not be. We can do them all at the same time. Gather them all together if you can, sort them into categories and then decide if they really have a place in your life anymore. Again, don't worry about what you are going to do with the discards when you are initially making the choices, just worry about handling them all and choosing positively what you are going to keep. Those that you are going to keep, give a good dust and then arrange back in their spots. I am not an interior designer, so my sole contribution to this will probably be – group in threes, I'm told that it looks good.

The discards for these categories I would suggest that you donate, or sell if they are really worth it, but remember the selling rules. Give yourself a date for them to be out of your home and if they are not gone by that date, donate instead.

Exercise Equipment

Some people have lots of exercise equipment in their homes, others have not so much. Yoga mats, kettlebells, whatever you have in your house that is meant to keep you fit. First of all, is it something that you are happy to have in your house? Do you use it – and I'm looking at that exercise bike that doubles as a clothes' stand here? Obviously, if the answer to either of those is yes, then I suggest you keep it.

I'm also going to say that if you don't use it right now, but in your Vision, you do, then hang on to it for now and return to it in 6 months' time when you've had a chance to bed-in with your new routine. However, if you bought that rowing machine a few years ago and now you realise that you just find rowing a completely boring pastime, let it go. It is usually easy enough to pass exercise equipment on to its next home through social media or neighbourhood groups/apps.

Living Area Summary

• Tapes degrade and will need digitising if you want to keep them	• Check wires and cables
	• Don't forget to wipe phones and computers
• Consider if you still have the ability to play the media	• Check out Terracycle for recycling
• CDs and DVDs can be stored in special bags to save space	• Schools may often take supplies
• Keep games accessible to encourage play	• Check wall art
	• Are all your pictures hung?
• Check pens and pencils	• Take ornaments out of their spot to assess
• Use the nice notebooks	
• Set up a Command Centre	• Consider if you use the exercise equipment
• Do a craft audit	

Living Area Worksheet

How do you feel about your living space(s)?	Describe your ideal living space.
What works?	What activities take place in here? What do you want to take place in here?
What doesn't?	What needs to change?
Where can you set up a Command Centre?	

Living Area Categories

Music	Electrical Equipment
• Vinyl	• Computers & peripherals
• Cassettes	• Printers & routers
• CDs	• Phones
Players (Film/TV)	• Gaming equipment
• Videos	• Music equipment
• DVDs	• Film equipment
• Blu-ray	• Cameras
• Other	• Wires – LET THEM ALL GO!
Office Supplies	**Crafting**
• Pens	• Tools
• Pencils	• Supplies
• Sharpeners	**Decorations**
• Rubbers	• Ornaments
• Rulers, protractors etc.	• Wall art
• Staplers, hole punches etc.	• Cushions & Throws
• Paper	**Other**
• Notebooks	• Exercise Equipment
Entertainment	• Furniture
• Family board games	
• Puzzles	

Chapter 11

Garage, Shed and Outdoor Spaces

I remember laughing one time at the horror in someone's tone as they said that most people couldn't fit their car into their garage. Well guess what? Neither can I! My garage is filled with hay and horse feed, much to Mr Tidy Coo's regret (as he'd like to put his car in it). Remember, as in all the categories that we do, it is your vision that counts, not anyone else's (well, Mr Tidy Coo's vision obviously does have impact in our household too...).

DIY and Tools

Tools are an interesting category because although they often do not bring joy in and of themselves, their practicality cannot be denied. Much better to have a decent hammer than to try to hang a picture by banging a nail in the wall with your shoe. However, as with so many practical things, they have a tendency to proliferate if you don't keep an eye on them because they are "useful". How many you will need will depend on the sort of property that you live in and how much maintenance you do yourself.

If you live in a serviced apartment in a city, the chances are that you will need precious little more than a screwdriver (if that), whereas if you live on an old, rural property which needs a lot of maintenance, you may find your tool requirements in this category to be somewhat higher. We live in the latter and, whilst neither of us pretends to be a whizz at DIY, we do have quite a number of tools.

As always, bring ALL of your tools into one place and sort them into subcategories. Go through each and work out how many of that type of tool you need and declutter accordingly. When it comes to storage, store like with like. For example, we have two quite large tool boxes in the garage, one which has the spanners and screwdrivers and other tools in, and one which has various glues and clamps in it.

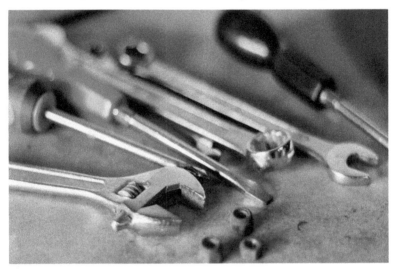

I do make a small exception for my like with like rule in this case. As our main toolboxes are in the garage, I have a mini box in the house that contains a hammer, ratchet screwdriver with various heads, a tape measure and a small selection of screws and so on. It stops me needing to make the trek out to the garage in the wind and rain and dark and it also means that small jobs, which are easy to do, actually get done as the tools are to hand in the house.

Include things such as car maintenance kits in this category.

Two micro categories are bulbs and batteries. Bulbs I include here because I remember being surprised by this category when going through our own ones, many of which had been left by the previous owners. I was amazed at how many we had that didn't fit any of the light fittings! Or perhaps were the wrong colour or shape to go with the rest of the bulbs on a fitting. Let these ones go! Often local social media groups are a good place to offload them to someone who actually uses them.

Another micro-category is batteries. This category is more about gathering them together in one place so that you know where to find them when you need them, but do check if they work before storing. Most councils will take used batteries or bulbs for recycling, but often require them to be in a particular bag on top of your bin. Otherwise, various supermarkets will also take them.

Decorating Equipment

Ferret round and bring out all the kit that you use when decorating — paints, brushes, rollers, sanding paper, filler, white spirit — anything that you need to get hold of when you are decorating a room. Then divide it into categories and go through it. Be pretty ruthless with this category, don't hang on to old paint for too long as it can go "off" quite badly (as I found out when I was painting the cabinet in my Utility recently!). Old paint usually needs to be recycled in a special area at the recycling centre, so make sure that you know the rules at yours.

With old paint brushes, do make sure that you only keep the best ones. Again, as I found out when painting my Utility room, you want to make sure that your brushes are up to the job. I was cursing at the quality of the paint I was using, when I came to realise it was actually the fault of the old brush that I was using. Once I picked out a better brush, the paint went on much better. Let those old brushes go: even properly cleaned, there is often only a certain number of times you can use them.

Once you have let go of the items that you do not wish to keep, make sure that you store the rest of the items together. Create sections or modules. I have boxes in my garage which are divided into kits. All my painting kit is in one, so I know that if I want to paint something, that I will find all the bits together, in one place, which always makes life easier!

Gardening

Gardening is not a passion of mine. I love a pretty garden and I love looking at flowers, or pulling home grown produce out of the ground, but getting them in there is a bit of a problem for me. With children, dogs, cats, poultry and, occasionally, horses running around the garden, we are not the sort of family who have stripes in our lawn (much to Mr Tidy Coo's eternal regret).

However, I still do grow things when I have the time and I have a range of implements that I use. Recently when I was having a big garage clear out and tidy, I pulled all my gardening stuff into one place. The pots, the tools, the bags of compost, the seeds, the gloves and I went through them. I checked to see what was broken and needed to be mended, what was broken beyond repair, what I no longer used, and most importantly, what made a positive impact on my life because it was used and useful. I organised for the broken stuff to be mended (although this is stretching the truth a little, because actually my mother organised for it to be mended), for the discards to be recycled or given away and the remaining items to be stored by category.

Camping

Until 2019, camping something that happened to other people, but then I started taking my horses to competitions that lasted more than one day. I needed kit to allow me to stay overnight in my trailer and after we made it on to the Scottish Endurance Riding Team for the Home International/Celtic Challenge, we needed to camp for a week as a family. Off we went and acquired a 6-person tent. We had enough camping chairs for all of us and I had already bought a camping stove and "kitchen", so we were pretty set. Whilst the riding was a highlight, I can't say that camping in a tent in mid-Wales in October was the best experience of my life, but having the right equipment certainly helped (as did half a case of Prosecco).

You know the drill by now – gather all of your camping equipment together and go through it. Inspect tents and ground sheets for holes, sleeping bags and mats for warmth and comfort and other equipment that you may have for usefulness and assess its general state of repair. Ensure that all your equipment is stored together and in a dry place free from damp and do check you have enough tent pegs!

Outdoor Living

This one includes barbecuing equipment, outdoor chairs, crockery that is only used outdoors etc. Again, bring each category together and check that it adds positively to your life.

Outdoor Toys/Leisure Equipment

This obviously includes children's toys, but there are plenty of things, like hot tubs and hammocks, that fit this category regardless of whether you have children or not. Include things such as bikes and scooters as well.

Remember to gather together the entire category to go through it, although I appreciate that you won't want to be moving the large equipment like trampolines.

I mentioned creating sections or modules for storing things like DIY supplies, and the same sort of idea can be applied to the outside space as a whole. Consider what activities take place out here and how you might like to zone them. For example, an area for outdoor dining and an area for children's play.

Garage and Outdoor Spaces Summary

• Practical things tend to proliferate	• Create sections or modules for storage
• It's not useful if you don't use it	• Consider zoning into areas

Garage and Outdoor Spaces Worksheet

How do you feel about your outdoor spaces?	Describe your ideal outdoor space.
What works?	What activities currently take place out here?
What doesn't?	What do you want to take place in here?
What needs to change?	What Zones would be useful?

Garage and Outdoor Spaces Checklist

○ Tool box	○ Seeds and plants
○ Hand held tools	○ Hot tub or pool equipment
○ Power tools	○ Camping equipment
○ Screw and fixings	☐ Tents
○ Bulbs	☐ Sleeping bags and mats
○ Batteries	☐ Chairs
○ Painting & Decorating equipment	○ Barbeque
	○ Barbeque equipment
○ Paints	○ Bikes
○ Gardening tools	○ Scooters
○ Pots	

Chapter 12

Longer Term Storage Spaces and Travel

Longer term storage spaces includes areas like a loft or attic. We don't have a loft space in this house, but we still have the categories that I will mention, so don't skip them!

If you do have an attic, I would really recommend putting some flooring down in it to make it easily accessible. The attic should not become a place to go for things which you can't make a decision on like old electronics, or broken furniture, but for things that need to go into slightly deeper storage, like seasonal and birthday decorations, luggage, and (occasionally) things that need to be kept between children, such as clothes. It should not be used as a storage space for photos and important documents – these should be stored in the main home because there is less risk of damage as the temperature and humidity is more regulated.

Remember to store like with like particularly in this area as things can have a tendency to be thrown in together which then makes it difficult to find them when they are needed.

Seasonal Decorations

I check my decorations when I get them out and when I put them away again. Generally, if I don't want to use a decoration when I get them all out, I ask why and if it is because it no longer makes me smile, then I let it go at that point. Then I check again as I put them away. Mainly at this point I am looking for breakages, or for stuff that my kids have made to put up that will not survive to the next year. I pack it up safely and store it. In this category, check that seasonal lights work.

Travel and Suitcases

Check your suitcases. See how many you have and whether or not they are in good working order – particularly check the stitching and zips. We used to have all sorts of hard-shelled cases, but unfortunately, once they were packed, they tended to exceed airlines' weight allowances, so we moved to lighter soft-sided ones. If you are discarding suitcases and other bags, do make sure to check them thoroughly! My husband found a pair of cufflinks that his late Grandfather had given him, that he thought he had lost, in the pocket of a suitcase.

Whilst we are on suitcases, we'll go into travel and packing. As we have been going through your home, I have encouraged you to collect all your travel stuff together wherever you have encountered it. Items like clothing that is only worn on holidays, holiday toiletries and other travel items such as eye masks and neck pillows.

Now is the time to go through it and to check that you have the right numbers and that they are all necessary. I suggest that these are kept together and preferably with your suitcases so that you are not hunting around the home when it's time for your holiday.

Pack Like a Pro!

Preparation

The key to a well-packed suitcase is preparation. I have a packing list so that I don't forget anything important. Although it has changed over the years, the change has been relatively gradual, and the list has gently evolved. The first thing that I do is to check the list and edit it according to what type of holiday we are going on. I remove anything from it that we don't need. I also have a look at the holiday and sketch out a plan of what we might be up to each day. Then I gather everything that I need for the holiday and bring it all together in to one place.

Minimise

I try to pack the absolute minimum that I can get away with. I like to travel light and have a manageable amount of stuff, but also, with four children, we all have to pack as little as we can get away with so that we can fit in the car. To that end, I often decant large toiletries into smaller bottles to take up less space. I also choose clothes that can be worn as part of several different outfits. It's like travelling with a mini capsule wardrobe.

Fold into outfits

Once I have gathered everything together, it's time to actually pack. I like to fold clothes in to outfits, based on what I might be up to on the various days, and pack the things that I will need first at the top of the suitcase. If I am wearing something twice, then I will pack it in the first outfit.

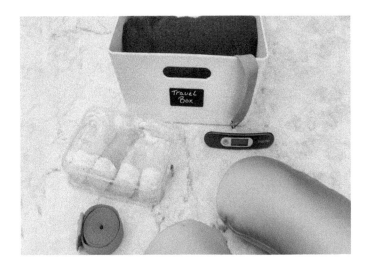

Longer Term Storage Spaces and Travel Summary

• Consider flooring attic spaces for safety and convenience	• Check suitcases for suitability
	• Check pockets before donating
• Do not store important documents or photos here	• Pack like a Pro
• Zone the area	▪ Prepare
	▪ Minimise
• Check seasonal decorations when they come out and when they go back away	▪ Outfits

Longer Term Storage Spaces Worksheet

How do you feel about your longer term storage spaces?	Describe your ideal longer term storage space.
What works?	What is currently stored here?
What doesn't?	What do you want to store here?
What needs to change?	What Zones would be useful?

Longer Term Storage Spaces and Travel Checklist

Seasonal	Travel
○ Lights	○ Suitcases
○ Christmas tree	○ Toiletries
○ Tree decorations	○ Travel towels
○ House decorations	○ Holiday clothing
○ Other seasonal decorations	○ Other

Chapter 13

Papers

I love doing paperwork with my clients because I can see what a huge difference it makes to their lives. It's often a huge mental barrier, but once it's cleared the relief is amazing. However, I've left them until almost the end of the book because people often get stuck here.

Gather

For paperwork, you will need to find yourself a flat, clear space to work in. A table that you can spread out onto is ideal, but I often end up on the floor in my clients' homes.

Some suggest that you should only touch each piece of paper once, but I think that if you are overwhelmed with papers, then this doesn't work because it is too much processing to do, so I recommend that we break it down into smaller steps.

First, gather papers from all over your home and bring them into one space. If you are doing this category towards the end of your journey, then you have been gathering them from all around the house as you have found them.

Declutter

Once you have them all together, you will need to handle every single piece to check which pile it needs to go into and you will need to make decisions on this as we go.

We're looking at four piles here, papers that can just be discarded straight into the recycling, papers that have personal information on that need shredding or burning, papers that need an action taken before it can be filed – this is the pending pile – and then papers to be filed. Do not break your heart over organising the stuff to be filed, broad categories are fine at this point. For example, bills, receipts, pensions paperwork, certificates and passports, manuals, newspaper clippings etc. Do not over categorise, or get caught up in trying to order things by date at this point.

Some specific questions for a few of the subcategories in the pending or file piles follow, to help you work through them.

Reference Papers

Will you refer to them again? Particularly for courses you go on. For example, I still frequently refer back to my notes on anything to do with Professional Organising (I'm always learning), but I have definitely ditched the revision notes that I made for my degree in Genetics that I took over 20 years ago. I often look at notes I made for teaching my kids, but have discarded all the notes I made for teaching other people's children.

Manuals

Do you still have the original item? It is not unusual for me to find old manuals in households where the item they are referring to has already been discarded. Even if you still have the item, ask yourself whether you really need to keep the manual, or whether you would look for the information online? We only have a couple of manuals now, mainly for things that are so old that they don't appear on the internet. A folder for manuals is a good idea, and whenever you put a new one in, make sure that you have removed any that you no longer need.

Guarantees

Check whether they are still in date and whether you have the necessary receipt to go with them. You will need a file for them with the guarantees filed in the order that they expire. Every time you come to file a new one, you can check to see whether or not there are any that you can discard. You can store these with the manuals, or on their own, but the trick to an Easy Life is definitely to check the old ones as the new ones come in. It gives you a reason and it's simple.

Bills

If you've paid them, do you need them any longer? Especially when everything is usually available online? Obviously if you decide that you do, you will need to decide how long you are going to keep them, because there is usually a pretty limited length of time that they will be relevant for.

Magazine Clippings

I come across pages ripped from magazines fairly frequently. These should be brought together and gone through. First of all, ask yourself if you are truly going to use them and see what you can discard first. Remember, it is always easier to organise when you have fewer things. Once you have decided what you need to keep, put them into a folder so that you can access them easily.

Recipes are another thing that I find loose copies of. I have to say that Mr Tidy Coo is a fiend for this. He loves to cook (and I love to eat – a match made in heaven) and so he will see a recipe, print it out and then it floats around the house until it is captured. I have two designated recipe folders in this house. The first is mine with the few things that I like to cook in it. It's very ordered, not many things in it, and all the pieces of paper are laminated to protect them from being damaged when I'm cooking. My husband's folder, on the other hand, is huge and bursting at the seams with random bits of paper. However, at least it is all in one place and when I find a random recipe beside the printer, I know where to put it.

Lists

I find a great number of loose lists in homes. My suggestion for dealing with them is in the next chapter!

Sort and Store

Now that we have decluttered the papers to be filed, it's time to get on and file them. I make 6 broad files for this:

Frequent Use

Anything that needs to be referred to frequently. This is anything that you will need easy and frequent access to. For me, it's things like the ponies' passports, my organising notes and any manuals that I have decided to keep. Most things are in a filing cabinet that we inherited with the house, but some are stored elsewhere. For example, the ponies' passports are to hand in the kitchen drawer because I don't want to be traipsing through the house in wellies when I need them. Equally, when I have finished with the vet outside, I want to just pop them back, often whilst I'm covered in mud, and I'd rather not have to walk through the house. Things should ALWAYS be easy to put away, or they will build up on the sides.

Important Documents

Birth & Marriage Certificates for example. We have these in a grab-and-go folder. We started this when we lived overseas, when we needed more frequent access to these documents and in extreme circumstances potentially needed to be able to grab them in case of emergency evacuation. We brought together anything irreplaceable and put it in a folder and we keep it now so that in the event of a fire, for example, we can grab it on our way out of the house. It is worth investing in a fire and waterproof folder for this.

Limited Time

Anything that you need to keep, but for only a set length of time (such as tax documentation). For this limited time paperwork, I like to put an entire tax year together – everything that might be needed for referral, and then I like to file it with the date of destruction on it, so usually seven years in the UK. Then when that seven years is up, that year's entire folder can just be pulled out and destroyed without needing to check it again. I prefer to file like this rather than keeping all bank with bank and all bills with bills because it makes it easier to refer to anything that you might need from a particular year, and also because it makes it easy to discard at the end of a period.

Deep Archive

A subset of important documents and is anything that needs to be kept indefinitely, but does not need frequent access, such as building warrants. This should be kept in the main body of the house where the temperature and humidity is stable, but it can be kept out of the way, perhaps somewhere like the top of a cupboard. Again, a fireproof folder is useful for this.

Dream Folder

This folder is one that I added more recently. It is a folder for your dreams and things that remind you about them. Take it out to look at it every so often to remind yourself about what you might want to do in the future!

Store

How long you keep paperwork is for you to decide. If you are in the UK, for tax purposes HMRC advises two years for those who are employed and seven years if you are self-employed, but I am not a tax or financial adviser and if you are concerned, then you should seek advice from someone qualified in that field.

Away from tax specific documents, what you keep is also entirely up to you. I have some clients who feel safer keeping practically everything, from old phone bills to bank statements to the Terms & Conditions that come with bank or credit card statements. I have some who like to keep old bills so that they can compare what they paid previously to what they pay now, and then I have some who are more like me; bills get discarded pretty much as soon as they are paid and most paperwork (bank statements etc.) can be found online. It is whatever works for you.

The next step is to deal with your pending papers. I have left the pending papers until last because it's another area where people can easily get bogged down. Take a look at your pending pile. Any task that takes less than two minutes, do it now. Tasks that take longer than two minutes, you need to make sure that you write down the next step to be done for it and then either put time in your calendar to do it, or have it on your list for things that need to be done when you next have a moment (look at the next section for Time and Diary Management).

Deal with Future Papers

Your papers are now organised, your bills are up to date and you're feeling (rightly) pretty pleased with yourself. How are you going to keep it that way? First, move as much as you can online, for example, credit card and bank statements, bills etc. Most companies will happily offer this as it is cheaper for them.

Unsubscribe from catalogues and open your post over the recycling bin. I often collect my post from the postman, and the junk mail goes straight into my recycling bin; it doesn't even enter the house. Keep a pair of shredding scissors by the recycling bin to deal with any information that you want to recycle securely. Open all of your mail every day and see what needs to be acted upon and what needs to be filed. Put a system in place near where the post comes in so that you have a Pending and File tray and then put aside time every week to take a few minutes to go through it.

Papers Summary

• Gather all your papers together.	• Deal with the Pending pile.
• Sort into 4 piles; recycling; shredding; pending; filing.	• Deal with your Future papers.
• File the things that need to be kept; Frequent Use; Important Documents; Limited Time; Deep Archive.	• Useful Files: • Manual and Guarantee folder • Recipe folder • Grab and Go Folder

Papers Checklist:

○ Reference papers	○ Magazine clippings
○ Manuals	○ Recipes
○ Guarantees	○ Lists
○ Bills	

Papers Worksheet

How do you feel about your paperwork system?	Describe your ideal paperwork system
What works?	
What doesn't?	What files would be useful?
What needs to change?	What storage solution(s) would help?

Chapter 14

Digital Spaces

It is all too easy to forget about decluttering the digital spaces in your life. After all, they don't take up much physical space, but they do take up room in your head! A decluttered digital space will help you to use your time more efficiently.

Decluttering digital spaces follows the same principles as decluttering physical spaces. Declutter first, start with the easy wins, work in categories, check everything, choose positively what to keep, store like with like and keep surfaces clear (in this case, that means the desktop!)

Computer Decluttering

Start by going through whatever folder structure you have been using, bringing similar files together and check to see whether you are making a positive choice to keep them. Discard the unnecessary and then store like with like. If your computer is a bit messy, it may take time to go through all of your documents, but believe me when I say that this is a good use of your time. It will free up space on your computer AND in your head.

When it comes to organising your files, I like to keep a clear desktop and to use a system that I would describe as a waterfall. Pretty big, broad categories, trickling down to a specific document. I prefer not to have too many choices in any one of the levels as it makes it easier to see what I am doing.

Email Decluttering

It is not unusual to be overrun by emails and the first step here is to have a good clear out of your Inbox.

Categorise

Use the search function on your email to check by categories. For example, if you search for "Amazon" everything relating to that should pop up and you can decide what to do with it.

Discard

With emails, I discard almost everything. If I decide it is important, like a receipt that I can't find elsewhere, or a correspondence that I want to keep, I file it in one of my folders, but be aware that this can be a slippery slope too – don't blindly file, ensure that you really are only keeping what you need. For example, do I really need the receipt for a set of pencils that I bought? Or the books? Once they have arrived, I'm not going to send them back, so I might as well delete the receipt. I generally only hang on to digital receipts if I would hang on the physical version. Remember that all your Amazon orders, for example, are available online on your Amazon account, and this is often true with other online accounts.

Unsubscribe

Those Special Offer emails? For stuff that you don't need and really shouldn't be buying? Bin them – use the search function to find them all, highlight and then trash. Then, and this is the really important part, unsubscribe from those emails. I have just two or three emails now that come in with offers that I might consider, the rest have gone. The same with random newsletters – if I'm uninterested, they go. Unsubscribing is a huge part of email management.

File

If you really need to keep something, then you can file it within a SMALL number of folders. I listened to a talk once that suggested that rather than try to delete emails, you could literally just dump them in folders by year and this does have the advantage that it is quick! The thinking behind it was that you could use the search function of your email to find anything that you needed and that it kept your inbox manageable to just those things that you needed to do something about. This might be a solution that works for you – if it does, then great. Anything over 7 years old, delete.

Create a To Do list in your Calendar, not your Inbox. Using your Calendar for reminders rather than relying on your email will help keep your attention focussed on what matters to you and prevent distraction. I've expanded on this in the Time Management section.

Turn your desktop notifications off – don't be at the beck and call of everyone else! Remember that your Inbox is really just a competing list of everyone else's priorities, not yours. Set time aside to check your emails and don't do it apart from at those times. It will make you more efficient (I promise).

Phone Decluttering

With the advent of smartphones, it's easier than ever to be distracted on the go. You pick up your phone to check the weather forecast and emerge an hour later having been distracted by social media and still not sure what the weather is going to do later. As always here, start by decluttering apps that you don't need, particularly those that are hugely distracting, but don't actually add much to your life.

To organise your phone, aim to keep your space as clear as possible. Keeping the Home Screen clear can minimise distraction. If there is an app that you would like to use less frequently, "hide" it in a folder and bring those that you would like to use more towards the front.

This has a natural run-on to social media. Consider which platforms add to your life and which platforms you leave feeling sad. Ruthlessly curate your Newsfeeds!

As an aside, I no longer watch the News programmes. This does not mean that I do not keep up to date with what is going on in the world, but I prefer to read it on sources that I trust than incessantly consume it on social media and TV.

Digital Worksheet

How do you feel about your Digital Spaces?	Describe your ideal Digital life:
What works well?	List your devices:
What frustrates you?	
What needs to change?	What apps can you delete from your phone:

Digital Summary

• Digital does not take up much physical space, but plenty of mental space	• Turn notifications off
• Declutter first	• Use your Calendar not your Inbox for your To Do list
• Keep Desktops and Home Screens clear	• Delete apps that do not add to your life
• Use the search function for email	• Curate your Newsfeeds
• Unsubscribe from emails	• Read the news rather than watch it

Chapter 15

Time Organisation and Management

My life could be described as somewhat busy and I could be described as somewhat scatty. As I said in the introduction, I am not a naturally organised person, so I have had to come up with a way of keeping my life on track. It had to be simple, straightforward and realistic, not overwhelming and above all, easy. I have attempted many systems over the years and have finally found one that works well for me. I will describe it here in the hope that it may work for you too, or if it doesn't exactly, that you may be able to adjust it to make it work for you.

The first part of any Time Management work that I do with clients is the Brain Dump. Working on the basis that our brains are hopelessly overloaded, we must get things out of our head and written down so that we have the mental space to actually focus on the task in hand.

This means that when we are, for example, writing a chapter about Time Management, our brains are on-task and not floating off worrying about shopping lists, or if we have the time to do the Couch to 5k, or will we remember to book the dentist for the horses in September. One of the biggest lies that we tell ourselves is that we don't need to write something down because we will remember it, but this is simply not true. Leaving a task in our heads rather than writing it down just leads to us worrying about it at inopportune times. I know that I have my tasks pinned down in my notebook, so I can put them from my mind and focus on the task in hand.

I encourage you to get a pen and paper and just start by jotting down everything that is on your mind. This may take some time, and the first time you do this, it may feel overwhelming as you start to see it all, but do not panic! This is only the first step. I have had clients fill several sides of paper with this and take several hours to get it all out of their heads, but getting it out of your head and onto paper is important to free up the space in your mind and prevent mental paralysis. Don't worry about sorting it beautifully into categories, but if you are struggling to corral your thoughts, then some basic prompts might be: Me, Home, Work, Animals, Kids. Once these thoughts are securely on paper, you can sort them into categories that make more sense to you personally.

Next, look at your brain dump and start to work your way through it. For each item, first of all, decide if it's actually something that you want to get done! Over the years, I have become a bit ruthless with my To Do list. Just as I have decluttered my physical belongings, so I have decluttered my diary. If it is not adding to my life, is it really something that I need to do? Just like removing unnecessary things from my home has helped me to keep it tidier, removing unnecessary things from my diary has made it easier to manage my life. In the same way that it's almost impossible to keep a home tidy and organised when it has too many things in it, it's pretty much impossible to keep and stay organised when you have a diary that is stuffed full. The first step is to declutter.

For the items that you decide to keep on your list, decide what the very next step is that you need to do to move it forward. If that step is going to take less than two minutes, do it as you are going through the list, then write down the next step for it. If the next step is going to take longer than two minutes, then plan time in your diary to do it (covered in the next section).

Having got all your thoughts, tasks and actions out onto paper, the next step is to organise your planner or diary. Many people use the calendars in their phones or on their computers to manage their time but, whilst I use my digital calendar to make appointments and notes related to them, I do find that a pencil and paper method focuses my mind more. The act of having to move items from one page to another makes me more likely to actually get them done and helps me to be intentional with my time.

I remember, back when I used to use an electronic list, that I had something very simple sat on my To Do list for about six months. Then I moved to a paper diary-based planner, and whilst I didn't mind writing it in my diary the first time, as soon as I had to move it from one page to another, I just got up and did the task instead! I do still use my phone to make a note of tasks as I go along if I am out and about, but I always transfer them to my paper diary and then they actually get done. I never lose my paper diary because it is in constant use.

Originally when I started paper-based time management, I used Ryder Carrol's Bullet Journal Method. However, I have evolved my own system from this, removing some elements and replacing them with features of my own.

When I set up my planner, I use a journal with dotted pages that are numbered. You can use any notebook though, so long as it has up to thirty-two lines. Initially when I tried this out for the first time, to get past the whole, "I want this to look perfect and I'm afraid of ruining it" thing, I just used an old notebook that I had lying around. Then, as I became more confident, I moved on to a better quality one, but remember that this is a working document; it doesn't necessarily need to look beautiful and you are not going to "ruin" it by writing in it. There are many different notebooks set up to do this sort of thing, just make sure that it has a decent number of pages in it so that you are not swapping between books halfway through the year.

I have twelve double-page spreads at the front of my notebook for the months of the year. For each of these monthly spreads, on one page I have the days of the month written down (which is why I need at least thirty-two lines in my notebook), and on the other page I jot down notes for things that are month-specific, such as worming the dogs or birthdays.

I then leave fifty-four double-page spreads for the weeks as I go through (because the year rarely begins on a Monday or ends on a Sunday!). This is the second important part of my system and it is a visual diary. I do love a good list and being able to tick things off it as I go, but the problem with a To Do list is that it doesn't take into account how long tasks are going to take, where you are expecting to be, where you have to be to do them, or how important they are. Having a visual diary helps with this. It shows you when you are expecting to do things and how long you are expecting them to take. It's not set in stone or rigid, but it's a good framework that helps you to balance structure and flexibility. It can also help you in saying "no" to things when you can see that you already have as much in your diary as you want to do.

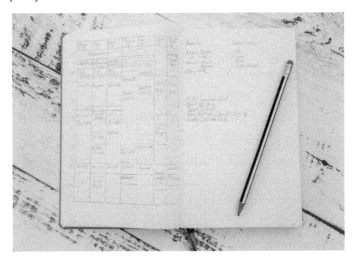

To set up my Visual Diary, I draw up my weekly grid and I start by writing in all my appointments and anything else that is set and booked. Then I look through my To Do list and I plan when I am going to get things done that week. Putting things into a specific slot helps me to be intentional and efficient with my time. I make sure that I leave free space in my day so that when the inevitable mishap arises (a traffic jam, a child hurting themselves, or a fence getting broken), I have time to deal with it and without a huge knock-on effect on the rest of my day. Be realistic with your time when you are doing this, remembering that things often take longer than we think, don't forget to plan breathing space for yourself. If you realise that you have too much to do in the time available, declutter your obligations.

At the end of each week, I take some time to review what I have got done (my Tah Dah List!) and what needs to be moved to a later date then I set up my diary for the coming week.

The other part of my planner is the index and note taking side of it which I referenced in the chapter on papers. Rather than covering various bits of paper in notes, and risk losing them, I keep all the notes together in my planner. For my notes, I start at the back of my notebook and write down everything that I need to remember, making a note of what page it is on in the index. For example, I like to make a note of any book titles that I want to read, keep a note of my budget, and write down packing lists. Each of these has a section in my planner, but the beauty of the system is that I don't have to worry about where I'm going to write them, I just go to the next available page and write on it, and then write down the page it is on in my index. This way, I can easily find whatever I need.

Like any decluttering and organising, this may take a lot of time the first time you do it, but once you have done it, it gets easier and quicker each time you do it.

Time Management Summary

• Our brains easily become overloaded	• Declutter your time and obligations as well as your physical belongings
• Writing things down helps clear our brain	• A visual diary can help with productivity and saying no
• Pencil and paper can be more effective than electronic	

Time Management Worksheet

How do you feel about your Time Management?	Describe how you would spend your time in an ideal week:
What works?	
What doesn't?	
What needs to change?	

Chapter 16

Children's Spaces

The very first thing to remember when working with children is that they often have very different priorities from our own. We may love certain toys, such as the beautiful wooden rainbows, whilst they hang on like grim death to the plastic toy that arrived stuck on the front of a magazine. What I say to people when I am working with their children is to focus on the end result. What do we want? We want children who grow into adults able to make decisions about what sort of lives they want to lead and what they want to surround themselves with. To that end, we really must allow children as much autonomy as possible in this area. If they feel confident that they are not being pushed to discard, then often they will discard far more. I am frequently amazed by the ability of children to make these decisions and I could provide example after example of confident children letting things go with ease once the pressure is taken off, but if you put the pressure on then they will not.

It may be worth starting with a good general pre-sort and tidy. When rooms get really untidy, it is just too overwhelming for the children to tidy them on their own. When my children's rooms get really untidy, we gather everything that is out into a pile on the floor. We sort it into categories on the floor and then we put them away.

Do not expect your children to be able to do this without being taught, so be sure to work alongside them as they learn these skills. Some children will learn the skills more quickly than others and others need support for longer. This is totally normal; after all, I work alongside adults who need varying degrees of my help, so why should children be any different?

One thing to think about when working with children is that it is super useful for them to have a space to call their own that is their own responsibility to keep tidy. This doesn't need to be their own room; it may just be a designated area within a shared room, or a toy chest in a living area, but do try and keep your own belongings out of their space. My youngest daughter has some amazing built-in cupboards in her room and, having no loft, we need to utilise this space, so two of the cupboards are "mine" and two of the cupboards are "hers". She knows she doesn't need to look into "my" cupboards and I keep my belongings out of hers.

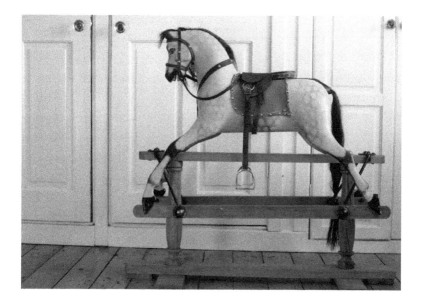

Children's Clothes

As always, let's not start by trying to tackle the difficult decisions, let's start with clothes. What fits? What makes them feel good? What do they like to wear? Again, I try to give my children as much autonomy as I can over how they dress and they really are so very different. My eldest loves to wear tracksuit bottoms and her favourite t-shirts all have holes in the sleeves. She loves for her hair to be tied neatly back in a French plait. My son is similar (minus the hair!), but my middle daughter definitely has a style of her own, with waistcoats and wild hair. My youngest would wear sparkly pink dresses for everything and loves nail varnish and makeup. I am really not sure where she gets that from, but I have tried to embrace it as far as possible.

Obviously, there will be clothes that they are not fond of that they have to keep, like school uniforms and perhaps one or two outfits for when they need to be smartly turned out. Even here though, I do try to get them to choose what their favourite smarter clothes are and work with those. Sometimes it helps children to let go if they know that their clothes are going on to a good cause, so I discuss who we might be passing these on to.

Once you have sorted their clothes with them, take some time to teach them how to fold their clothes properly. Remember that this is an art that takes time to learn, but it is worthwhile teaching it to them. My children have been folding their own laundry for years; when it comes off the line or out of the dryer, I sort it into baskets and then they fold it as part of their daily routine. Your children may well not initially do it as well as you would, but try to move past that. If you do it for them, all that they will learn is that you are better at doing it than they are.

On the subject of clothes and folding, as I mentioned in the chapter on laundry, each family member here has their own clean laundry basket and is responsible for folding their laundry. The clean laundry baskets are where odd socks live whilst waiting for their partner to come through the wash. It is the same with other items that need a partner to complete them, such as pyjama sets. This makes it easier for the kids to get dressed as everything is already in sets in their drawers, rather than trying to find something to match amongst everything else.

Children's Miscellaneous

Rather than jumping from clothes to toys, which is often quite a difficult category for children, we'll take a tour through their belongings that aren't clothes and aren't toys, such as stationery, books and papers.

I don't know about other people's children, but mine seem to breed these in their rooms; there are frequently piles of books on bedside tables and papers shoved into desks. Once again, remember that when working with children, we are focusing on the long-term goal of them being able to make decisions themselves, so if they are over the age of about three, please allow them as much autonomy over this process as possible.

Bring all of the items in a given category into a pile and get them to go through them one by one. Try to respect their decisions; if they want to discard something that you want to keep, then take that item into your own space rather than keeping it in their space. If you are doing books, as often they are held jointly, then you should ask each child to go through the books one after the other.

Old schoolwork is something that I often come across in homes. Involve your children in deciding if there is anything that they want to keep (spoiler alert – probably not).

I am frequently asked how I store children's artwork and my usual reply is, "In the bin!". Which is not to say that I always throw everything out; my kids like to keep special pieces in their rooms and I do love to be given drawings and artwork. Long term though, I only keep the ones that are very special. Mostly, once it has been finished and admired (and perhaps had a photo snapped of it), pictures are pretty much recycled (shredded and used as bedding for the rabbits) as soon as they are finished with.

Children's Toys and Games

Toys and games seem to be such a flash point in many homes I am in, but they really needn't be. Once again, try to remember to keep your eye on the long-term goal of raising children who know what they want in their lives. They may have very different priorities to you. I always used to love the wooden toys, but my kids always seemed to get attached to plastic tat instead. I try not to throw these things away without their permission, tempting though it is.

First of all have a chat to your children about why you are decluttering. It is worth pointing out to them that it is easier to keep things clean and tidy if you have fewer toys. Birthdays and Christmas can be useful prompts for a declutter because it can be seen as a time to make space for anything new that may come in.

I often remind my children how lucky they are to have what they have and how nice it is to give things away to children who are less fortunate than they are. If that doesn't work, then alternatively my children are always keen to earn some extra cash by selling some of the more expensive toys!

Don't feel too disheartened if this initial attempt at toys does not yield dramatic results. My younger two girls took four attempts, over the course of a couple of years, before they suddenly seemed to "get" it, and on that attempt SO many things went! It was as if they suddenly realised that they were in charge. On that occasion, it has to be said that they both had a pretty strong Vision because they wanted to make their bunk beds into single beds and there wasn't room to do so with the number of toys that they had. The golden rule here is to try not to take over the process; the more control that they can have, the better.

I will say that once, many years ago when my children were tiny, I was despairingly sorting through a pile of toys which they had dumped out of boxes on to the floor, and I had a bit of an epiphany. I realised that the toys that they had left on the floor were actually the toys that they didn't play with! They had emptied the box in search of a favourite and then run off with the favourite and left the rest on the floor. I was able to let this stuff go with no upset. If you have very small children, do watch for this behaviour as it can be a useful indication of what they actually like. Now that my children are older, the toys out on the floor tend to be the things that they are playing with and I don't remove their belongings without their absolute permission.

On to the actual declutter. Sort the toys into piles by type and then go through them one by one. As with their books, if there are communal toys, get each child to check individually and stress to them that they are picking for themselves, not worrying about what the other child wants to keep because the other will also get the chance to keep anything that they want to.

Storing Toys and Games

Once you have gone through the pile, it is time to think about storage for the toys. My general rule is to not have lids on anything. I like shelves with boxes that they can pull out, because they can just pull out the box, put the toy in and close it again. Somehow this seems to take less effort than opening a lidded box, as items often get piled on top of the lid. Make it obvious where things go; picture labels for young children are useful here. Whilst categorising is good, try to keep categories broad to make it simple to put things away. For Lego, I like to use shallow boxes or trays, so the bricks can be seen without having to scrabble through them. An alternative are those big drawstring bags that spread out for them to play, and then scoop up into a big bag. For what it's worth, I never sort Lego by colour, only by type. Much easier to find a yellow one-er in a box of one-ers than it is in a box of yellows!

Keeping It Tidy

I know that there are families out there who like to tidy as they go along, and if this works for you, then brilliant, because you are unlikely to get in such a mess. For us though, I prefer not to disturb the flow of play as my children move from one activity to another, so instead we have a tidy up time each day before they can get their tech out. Putting things away regularly like this means that it doesn't become overwhelming, but it will require input from an adult, at least initially. My kids are now old enough to do it on their own, but when they were younger, I would work alongside them, and I still do so if the house has become particularly untidy.

On a final note, remember that whilst we are aiming to get the children to take ownership of dealing with their own belongings once they are in the home, YOU are in charge of what comes into your home! Talk to relatives about the benefits of living with fewer toys – not only is there less to clear up, but it's also beneficial for play.

In our household, we really try to not go overboard at Christmas and on birthdays. We'll often ask relatives for money towards an activity or season tickets, instead of a physical gift. Or maybe for help towards buying sports equipment such as bikes, rather than another toy that will get lost in the pile. Talk it through with them; most people are happy with this approach once they know your priorities. This is a nice little rhyme I use to help keep gift buying under control:

Something they Want,

Something they Need,

Something to Wear,

Something to Read.

School and Routines

On the subject of children, I'd like to mention some routines around school. I am not a parenting expert, just a mother of four and I no longer send my children to school, as I Home Educate them, but I do remember the days of getting them ready for school. So now, although we don't have the scramble out of the door for school, I do still need to get my kids up and ready for the day every day.

The biggest thing here is that we want to take the stress out of life as much as possible. I may not have to get my kids out of bed for school, but I do like to be out walking the dogs together by 8am every morning, having had a calm breakfast beforehand.

The key to this is to set up a good routine. A calm morning starts the night before with laying out clothes and getting packed lunches ready, ideally your children should get in the habit of doing this themselves, with support to begin with, then on their own. A packed lunch station in the kitchen makes it easy for them to help themselves to what they need, and I talked about organising the food in your fridge and cupboards to make it easier for the children. Of course, you may still want to run your eyes over what they are taking out (on several occasions, I've stopped my son from taking out just half a piece of bread with some honey in it), but anything that means that you have less to do overall is a good thing. Packing their school bags up the night before as far as possible is also a useful thing to do.

A peaceful start to the day is important for all involved. My husband and I both get up an hour before the children and use this quiet time to prepare ourselves for the day before the children get up. I wake my children up pretty peacefully too – about half an hour before they need to get out of bed, I go into their rooms and open the curtains and turn on the lights. Daylight alarms are an excellent idea in this situation too, especially in the winter with darker mornings – it's always easier to get up in the light than in the dark. I like to read to my children over breakfast every morning for several reasons. One, we all enjoy it, two, it stops them arguing and three, it stops them dawdling.

Set up an area where their bags are stored and can be returned to every afternoon when they get home. When my kids were at school in Australia, I used to have an area in the garage where all their school stuff was kept (it even had a fridge for their lunches!). So when I sent them all off to get ready, they had everything in one place, including any sports kit. We put their homework there at the end of each evening too. I had a board on which the days that they needed their kit was written and anything else that was relevant for the day too. Try to carve out a space for something like this.

Empty those bags every day. Get your children into the habit of emptying their bags as they come through the door. Letters and papers put into a designated tray for you to look through, lunch boxes emptied and wrappers thrown away, sports kit straight into the washing basket. It's hard when everyone is tired, but worth getting used to doing.

Set up a Homework station so that they can easily get sorted. This can be in their bedrooms if they are more autonomous, or at a kitchen or dining table if they need more support. If you don't have a lot of space, the storage bags that go over the back of chairs are very useful for this. This then avoids having things spread throughout the home.

If you have tiny children coming home from school, make sure that you meet them with a snack! It's a long day for them. I know some parents who pretty much give their children their evening meal as soon as they are in through the door and then just a snack supper afterwards, which is as good an option as any. We try to eat as many meals together as a family as we can, if the evening meal is too difficult with activities and so on, then breakfast together is another good option.

Finally, whether your children have school lunches, or you are providing a packed lunch, a meal plan is super helpful. I talked about this in the Kitchen chapter. When we cook something like a Bolognese here, we almost always cook two or three times the amount we need and the rest can go in the freezer for days when everyone is in a rush.

Children's Summary

- Children's priorities are often different to our own

- Children need autonomy over their own space

- Children often need support just like adults do

- Children learn by watching – do your own journey first

- Progress over perfection

- Keep spaces defined

- If you want to keep an item that they wish to discard, take it into your own space.

- Folding clothing into sets helps with dressing

- Communal items should be checked by one and then the other

- Use simple labels and broad categories

- Avoid lids, drawers are easier

- You are in charge of what comes into your home

School

- Prepare the night before for an easier morning

- Have a "school" area for bags and supplies

- Set up a homework area

Children's Checklist

○	Tops	○	Bags
○	Bottoms	○	Jewellery
○	Dresses	○	Toiletries
○	Uniform	○	Stationery
○	Sportswear	○	Craft supplies
○	Nightwear	○	Note books
○	Underwear	○	Paper
○	Footwear	○	Drawings
○	Coats	○	Books
○	Hats	○	Toys
○	Scarves	○	Games

Children's Spaces Worksheet

How does your child feel about their space?	Ask your child to describe their ideal space.
What do they like about it?	What activities take place in this space?
What don't they like about it?	What do you both want to take place in here?
What needs to change?	Where can you set up a school supplies and homework area?

Chapter 17

Memories

Finally we come to memories and, in the next chapter, photos. This is quite a wide-ranging category, which can include clothing such as wedding dresses, jewellery, old teddies and toys, trophies and medals, children's artwork, your own artwork and so on. Split these into smaller categories before attempting to work on them and remember to try to work on an entire category at a time, however small that category might be.

There is no denying that this can be a tough category. Tears, both happy and sad, happen fairly frequently during this category when I am working with clients and it is important during this category to take breaks when it gets hard. Even if you power through it, take time to acknowledge your feelings and, if it gets overwhelming, take some time out, and do something that makes you feel happy. There have been times when I have been working with my own items when I've had to stop because the memories have become overwhelming. You don't have to do it all at once and remember, always start with the easy things first.

There are four questions that you need to ask yourself during this topic and I will go through them in greater detail. They are:

1. Do I love it?
2. Does someone else love it?

3. Is it important to someone else?

4. Is it of historical importance?

Do I love it?

The first is the most important question and will decide if it lives in your home or not. If you don't love it, then do consider the other three questions first, before you let it go.

Does someone else love it?

You can offer these things to the people for whom they may bring joy, but be sure to reassure the person to whom they are being offered that they can turn them down without causing offence. An example of this could be offering back letters to someone – my mum found all the letters that she had written to my grandmother when living overseas. She's been really happy to read these again and has considered putting them into a book.

Children's drawings also go into this category. Do include your children in deciding what they would like to keep and what they would like to let go of, and make sure you have read the chapter about working with children first. You can make all sorts of things with these drawings if you decide to keep them.

Is this of importance for someone else?

The third question is, "Is this of importance for someone else?". These items may be tricky, and they are generally things that may be of importance to children or other younger relatives in the future. I'm not so much talking about artwork and school reports, but documents related to family history that you think it may be important for them to know in the future, or photos and so on. Things that may be difficult for YOU, especially in the case of divorce or bereavement, but which are an important part of their own history. I would store all these together in an archival quality box and then put it in a spot that is out of sight for you, such as the top of a cupboard, so that you are not having difficult memories continually triggered. Hand it on as soon as it becomes appropriate.

Is this of historical importance?

The last question is, "Is this of Historical Importance?". Sometimes things that do not feel relevant or important for you or your family any longer may be of importance to other people. One of my lovely long-standing clients, who was at the forefront of the local Feminist movement has many fascinating things that we offered to the Glasgow Women's Library. Another client has old magazines which we contacted the local Archivist about, to see if they would like them. If you are not sure if they are historically important, your local Archivist should know and you can contact them through your Local Authority. The Archivist is usually attached to libraries or museums.

Finally, this is not a question as such, but more of a thought when it comes to discarding memorabilia. Sometimes things can be worth quite a lot of money so, even though I'm usually totally up for donation, don't throw the baby out with the bathwater here. You may want to consider getting particular items valued by a specialist. However, do not hang on to things just because they might be valuable unless you have specifically bought them for that purpose. For example, one of my clients collects special edition coins with the intention that it's actually a saving for the future.

If an item does not tick any of these boxes, then it is time to let it go. Do so with a light heart, but just because it doesn't tick a box, doesn't mean it's easy.

Sometimes we can find it difficult to part with things that trigger our memories but that we don't love. Maybe looking at it hurts our heart, or perhaps we are keeping it because we feel we ought to. I worked with a client who had been keeping a skirt that belonged to her sister. She felt that she ought to hold on to it because her mother had. However, her sister hadn't wanted to keep it and when I asked the question, "Do you love it?" she looked at it with a little surprise and admitted that she didn't and that in fact it made her heart hurt because it represented a loss. I suggested that she release it for another person to find joy with, someone without the emotions attached to it, and she did.

Other times, we hang on to large bulky things in order to try to preserve a memory, but often there are smaller ways that work just as well as memory prompts. Remember that it is always possible to take a photo. There are people who will do it for you if you'd like a really good one. Over the years I have been fortunate to receive several large trophies for my horse riding, but I have been even more fortunate that I have had to give them back after my year is up! I have taken a good photo of them as a reminder before letting them go.

Trophies and medals – those who compete in sports will often end up with quite a collection of ribbons or rosettes. In each season I display all those that I have won in my front porch, but at the end of the season I look through and only keep the most special. Letting go of the rosettes doesn't mean that I am letting go of the competition or the time I spent preparing for it, it's just a physical memento and I get so many of them that it's not worth hanging on to the ones that aren't special. Sometimes I'll turn down a rosette so as to cut down on waste if I know that I won't keep it.

Honouring Cherished Things

Enjoy this storage category! Once you have decided you want to keep a particular object, think about how you are going to honour it. There is no point in hanging on to things and shoving them in the back of a cupboard never to be seen again. Consider getting sentimental jewellery re-set if you won't wear it in its current form.

Wedding dresses can be beautifully boxed up if you wish to keep them, or let go to charity, or given to a charity that makes gowns for stillborn babies.

A quick note about Archival Storage is relevant here. Everything physical degrades; there is nothing that we can do to stop this process. We can, however, slow it down. Make sure that things that you love are well-preserved in acid-free storage within the main home, but there are so many ways that you can store and display these memory items so that your happy memories can be enjoyed every time you see the items. Your only limit is your imagination!

One storage solution that I often use for clients' cards is a hexagonal display. You use a special cutter to put it into books or pictures. Other people make garlands out of Christmas cards.

Consider your Legacy

None of us like to think about dying, but the fact is that we all will. "The Gentle Art of Swedish Death Cleaning" by Margareta Magnusson is a book I love for its no-nonsense and pragmatic advice on this subject and I specifically want to mention two topics here. Everyone has a history; for some people it is more complicated than others. I like Margareta's advice about your own history which is, "If you think that the secrets will cause your loved ones harm or unhappiness, then make sure to destroy them".

My advice is if you cannot bring yourself to destroy them, to keep them in a locked box to which a trusted friend has the combination (label on the box that it is to go to this friend). Obviously make sure that your friend is in agreement with this and, when you pass on, they will be able to make sure that they destroy the contents of the box.

The second topic that I would like to touch on is that sometimes we keep stuff just for ourselves which is probably meaningless for someone else, but equally, it's not going to cause harm. For example, I have some silly pictures of stick people that I drew when I was doing a lot of yoga and I wanted to remember the poses and sequences. You can label a folder up for this with something like, "Unimportant - feel free to burn without looking". Then it's up to them whether they look or not. I would not use this method for possible harmful things though.

My final piece of advice is to give yourself time and space for this category, it can be hard work!

Memories Summary

The 4 questions:	
1. Do I love it?	3. Is it important to someone else?
2. Does someone else love it?	4. Is it of Historical importance?

Memories Worksheet

How do you feel about your mementos at the moment?	How would your mementos be stored and displayed ideally?
What works?	
What doesn't?	What supplies do you need?
What needs to change?	

Memories Checklist

o Clothing (wedding dresses etc.)	o Letters
o Childhood toys	o Cards
o Childhood drawings	o Certificates
o Trophies and medals	o Other
o Jewellery	

Chapter 18

Photo Organising

As well as training and certifying as a KonMari Consultant, I have also trained as a Photo Manager and this chapter is written from that perspective.

It is entirely normal for me to come across photo collections that are completely out of control. Just like CDs and DVDs, this is an area where your age will be likely to determine how many physical vs digital photos you have.

We take more photos every minute or two than existed in total a hundred and fifty years ago. Whilst this enormous boom has led to fantastic ways to record lives, it has also led to overwhelm. One of my first Photo Management Clients had over forty thousand photos on her phone (and I have had workshop attendees with over ninety thousand). Whilst every part of her amazing life was recorded, she had no easy way to access the most important memories. Twenty hours of intense work later, I had halved the number and backed up the remainder so that we at least had digital copies.

But digital copies and digital photos are rarely enough, as photos are at their best when we can share them with each other and that is easiest to do in a physical form. My children love to look through the photobooks that I have made.

Preparation

As with all of our categories, we first need to work on our vision, because a strong vision will help you through when it becomes a slog – which it definitely will do at times.

The next step is to make a note of all the family history we know, dates of birth, wedding dates, graduation dates, important holiday dates and so on, as this will make the actual sorting process so much easier. Gather your supplies together (there is a list in the worksheet) and prepare the area you where will be working. You will need a large flat area, preferably where you can leave things out for some time as this is not necessarily a quick job. Bear in mind that oil from your fingers can damage photos, so I recommend wearing cotton or nitrile gloves if you can.

Gather

Then we need to gather photos together. For the physical photos look in attic, wardrobes, bedrooms, cellars, cabinets, cupboards, drawers, on the walls, under beds, storage units, storage bins, on the refrigerator and in the garage. For the digital photos look for external hard drives, smartphones, tablets, cameras and of course computers, as well as social media and any online storage accounts that you may have. At this point, try to just collect rather than get caught up reminiscing! There are so many places you can look, do check them all as there is nothing more frustrating than finding an extra set of photos that you didn't know you had and trying to fit them in to your display.

Digital photos are more at risk than physical photos so anything that is on your computer should be backed up on to a hard drive to prevent loss as soon as possible.

Sort

Remove photos from non-archival storage such as sticky or magnetic albums and sort as chronologically as you are able, using the notes on family history that you made in the beginning. Then go through and look for the photos that tell your story, choosing positively the ones that you love. These photos are the ones that are going to go into your albums, or on your wall. There may be other photos that you don't love as much as these, but that you want to keep, and you can store these in archival quality boxes. As with mementoes, these boxes should be stored in the main body of the home where the temperature and humidity are relatively stable, not in the attic or garage.

So far, I haven't told you which things you ought to discard, but I'm going to go out on a limb here. Discard your blurred photos, any duplicates, random unidentifiable landscapes and shots of your food. Thank these and send them on their way! As an example, here in Aberdeenshire we get the most amazing sunsets and I always hop outside and try to capture them on my phone. I'm not always successful, but enough of them are that I have a fair amount. When I go through these I am only keeping the most spectacular. Similarly, I take hundreds of photos of my girls and me out riding. I don't need to keep them all, I can let go of most of them. Pictures of my animals too;

there only so many photos I need of my big dog pulling his funny face, or my small one with her head under my pillow. By trimming down only to the best, I'm able to share them more easily and the remaining photos have far more impact.

I've spoken about ordering your photos chronologically but although we live chronologically, we remember by event, so how you will arrange your photos is up to you. Think about how you are likely to want to retrieve them. What are the themes of your life; is it celebrations, or animals, or holidays?

Save

Why should you scan? I mentioned in the chapter on Memories that all physical items degrade, and this is particularly true of photos. Whilst we can slow this degradation down, we cannot stop it. Digitising photos helps us to preserve them in the longer term (although it is worth remembering that hard drives also need to be upgraded regularly). Creating a digital copy can help you to share things more easily with friends and family. You can also add a lot of information to digital photos in the form of metadata and tags, such as location and dates. Scanned photos can be enhanced in applications like Light Room with silvering taken off and colour corrected.

When it comes to the saving and scanning part, you can include the things that we worked on in the last chapter. Things such as children's artwork can be scanned or have a photo taken of it. You can also photograph objects – I mentioned that I photograph the trophies that I win before I have to hand them back. It is not always necessary to keep a physical reminder when a photographic one will do. Alternatively, it may be that you want to keep the little first shoes tucked away in a memory box, but it would be nice to put a picture of them in the album that you'll look at regularly.

For scanning photos, I recommend scanning prints at the highest quality that you can. When scanning it is important to keep things clean. Remove dust and debris from the scanning surfaces and also from the surfaces of the photos you are scanning. A microfibre cloth can be used to clean the glass of a scanner and can also be used on the photos themselves. Transferring VHS and other tapes is harder at home yourself and you are best to get a professional to do this for you. If you aren't confident scanning photos, then there are plenty of professionals who offer this as a service.

Once you have everything safely digitised, you need to look at back up. Digital photos are at risk, so anything that you have decided is worth keeping a digital copy of ideally should be backed up three times, on two types of media with one stored off site. So you may have a copy on your computer, a copy on a hard drive and a copy in a cloud-based account. That way, your photos are safe, even if there is a fire and you lose the originals, or you lose access to the cloud copy.

A word of warning here about iCloud. Whilst cloud-based storage is an excellent backup; for example Drop Box, Google photos, Amazon photos and similar, iCloud is NOT a backup! iCloud is a brilliant and powerful synchronisation tool, but I have had clients who have lost all of their photos through deleting on their phones and then discovering that they have deleted their entire collection. If discovered in time, the collection can be recovered, but if you press "Permanently delete", it is gone for good. For ever. There is no way to retrieve it. So please do not treat iCloud as a backup, deleting photos from your phone and expecting Apple to have a backup, because they won't have one!

As far as external hard drives go, you need one that is a decent size in order to be able to take all your back-ups. Once you have scanned, you will be able to estimate the minimum size required, but in general I wouldn't buy one less than 1 TB. Err on the side of greater capacity, bearing in mind that your collection, and therefore your back-up requirements, will only grow.

Share

This is the fun bit and there are so many options out there! Celebrate your family legacy and print photobooks, make video slideshows and online galleries, and get those photos framed. Print out that family recipe book. You will not for one minute regret the time and energy you put into this.

On an end note, I have had some clients who prefer to go fully digital and I do understand the reasons behind doing this, but for me there is nothing quite like having photos printed out into albums. Like everything else, your solution should work for you.

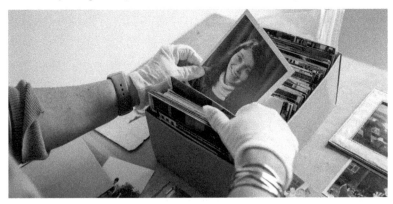

Photos Worksheet

Supplies:	
• Large area to work on • Dental floss or craft spatula for removing photos from albums • Sticky notes or index cards to label piles of photos • Camera and notebook for taking notes	• Storage containers with dividers for sorting • Gloves to protect the photos and mask to protect yourself from dust • Bin Bag

How do you currently feel about your photos?	How would your photos be stored and displayed ideally?
What works?	
What doesn't?	What needs to change?

Photos Checklist

Places to Search	Looking for
o Attic	o Tablets
o Wardrobes	o Cameras
o Bedrooms	o Online accounts
o Cellars	o Loose printed
o Cabinets	o Photo albums
o Drawers	o Scrap books
o· Walls/table tops	o Artwork
o Under beds	o Report cards
o Offsite Storage units	o Documents
o Storage bins	o Certificates
o Refrigerator door	o Heirlooms
o Garage	o Frames
o External hard drives	o Trophies and medals
o Computers	o DVDs
o Smartphones	o CDs
	o Memory cads
	o Computer images
	o Smartphone images
	o Anything you want to document digitally

Chapter 19

Storage and Finishing

Well done for getting this far! Hopefully you've worked through the chapters and have decluttered and are now ready to look at your storage solutions. But before we do, let's first of all go back and remember why you were doing this. You picked up this book because you were looking for ways to make your life easier. Maybe you felt overwhelmed and out of control. That your home was taking up too much of your time and energy and was not the peaceful sanctuary that you had hoped that it would be when you moved into it.

We are aiming for a home that is filled only with the things that you love, only with the things that support you in the life you want to live. Maybe that home has lots of things in it, because lots of things makes you feel safer, or maybe it's a home with very little in it, because fewer things makes you feel calmer. With the one proviso that it is easier to keep things under control when there are fewer things, remember that this is not about right or wrong numbers, but about what works for you and makes your life easier. However, if you are struggling to keep your possessions in order, continue to declutter until it becomes easy. Whatever your vision was, revisit it frequently and make sure that it's still what you want.

Storage

Once you have fully decluttered, it is a good opportunity to take some time to finesse your storage solutions. I have mentioned some of these as we have gone along, but I'm just going to bring them together in one place.

- A place for everything and everything in its place. Everything MUST have somewhere that is its designated home so if it hasn't got one, give it one now.
- If you are not sure where to put something, try asking yourself where you would look for it and make its home there.
- Keep surfaces clear; it makes all the difference for lines of sight and ease of cleaning.
- Like with Like – don't have stuff spread all over your home so that you're not sure where to look for it. Keep things together.
- Use smaller containers to corral items in larger spaces. These can be either boxes that you already had or, if you have finished your journey, now is the time to buy new ones if you wish to.
- Drawers are more useful than boxes with lids.
- Use vertical storage and store vertically. Remember that the backs of doors are helpful, and file fold or store so that when you open a drawer, it can all be seen easily.
- Heavier things should go at the bottom, lighter towards the top, it will save your back.
- Things that are used most frequently should be in the prime spaces – easiest to reach and should also be easy to put away.
- Colour coding and labels are super useful; make labels fun if it helps – like "Things that should have been done yesterday".
- Make sure that the place of honour in the room holds something that truly brings you happiness and makes you smile.

Finishing off

There comes a time in our homes when we look around the room and it seems "done". However, sometimes everything in the room might seem like you love it, but the room still isn't quite there. Sometimes the answer is to remove something else – perhaps a piece of furniture, or make sure that the sides are clear. Sometimes the answer is to rearrange the room – perhaps the flow of the room is being impeded by an item. Sometimes the answer is to add something!

People can get a little bit over enthusiastic about decluttering. You start and you see how much easier your life is without all of this stuff and you can go a little to the other side of it. This is totally fine and normal.

Just remember that you can't be happy by removal alone; you have to choose what to keep in your life, and sometimes that involves adding something. I remember being stood in a room with a client and we knew that the room wasn't right. It was a dining room, but it had the printer in it as that was the most convenient space to have it. I surveyed the room, stood back and then pointed towards the sideboard and said, "A small piece of furniture there is what you need, so that you can put the printer on it". So off my client went, found a side table that wasn't in use, put it in the spot, with the printer on it and the supplies in it and boom, it was perfect. It was lower than the sideboard, so the printer was below the sweep of the eye.

So sometimes we need to add to our spaces, and in this situation a mindful shopping list can be helpful, like I talked about in the capsule wardrobe section. Life is not static: just because something is perfect right now does not always mean that it will remain so, but be aware of change for change's sake.

Chapter 20

Maintaining Your Easy Life

So now that you've set up your Easy Life, how do you maintain it?

I do this in two main ways. The first is to rigorously apply the principles I set out in the Time Management chapter, and the second is that I refresh my home twice a year. I do this refresh because life is not static: I still buy things, stuff wears out and priorities change. With each refresh, the easier I find it to let things go. The more I let go, the easier I find it to live.

To do a refresh I revisit my vision and then work through the categories one by one, checking that the items I have still support me. As I go through this, I also make a note of any gaps that might have appeared and add these to my mindful shopping list. I also note any maintenance that needs doing. The refresh doesn't take me long because our possessions are already decluttered and categorised and it is definitely worth the time it takes.

I am so busy in my day to day life that I don't have time to be faffing about looking for things or fixing things that go wrong. I need my life to run smoothly and to be easy and I don't want to be spending my life tidying up and organising – unless, that is, it's helping other people! Instead I want to spend my life riding my horses, playing with my children and spending time with my husband. I want to live an Easy Life and I want to do it with minimal effort.

Finally, as we reach the end of this book, I hope that you have found the advice to be useful and feel inspired to declutter, organise and finally live an Easy Life. As I said at the beginning of this book, getting organised is all about making your life easier. It's about having the time to do the things that make your heart sing. It's an investment of your time now, to make your future life easier. Remember organised people are just too lazy to look for things! Above all, I am not organised because I have time; I have time because I am organised.

Six-monthly Maintenance – Spring and Autumn

• Check Vision	• Check Use by and opening dates
• Go through all categories	• Go through paperwork
• Handle everything	• Remove excess wires
• Check for broken or damaged items	• Check car
• Check for fit	• Make a mindful shopping list for the home
• Check for duplicates	• Clear the surfaces
• Do maintenance for storage	• Clean before you put things back
• Wash make-up brushes	• Return every item to its home, if it doesn't have a home, make it one.
• Oil tools	
• Completely empty bags and pockets	

Book maintenance tasks:

• Sweep chimneys	• Clear gutters
• Order winter fuel	• Lag pipes
• Order winter salt	• Anchor trampolines

About the Author

Rosie Barron is an award-winning Professional Declutterer and Organiser and founder of The Tidy Coo, who lives in Aberdeenshire with her husband and their four Home Educated children and a whole menagerie of animals including ponies, dogs, cats, bunnies, poultry and fish. Clearly not a minimalist.

As a child, Rosie moved around the world with her parents, living in Africa, Asia and the Caribbean. After leaving University and working as a Cytogeneticist, Rosie trained to be a Primary school teacher and worked in schools in the UK and Italy before taking time out to have a family. She continued moving internationally, to India and Australia, with her young family, finally settling in Aberdeenshire in 2017.

In 2018, inspired by years of moving home and seeing how being decluttered and organised helped her to keep her full life on track, Rosie trained to be a Professional Organiser and set up The Tidy Coo. She loves the breadth and scope of the work and the impact that getting decluttered and organised has on her clients.

www.thetidycoo.com